Fluency in Number Facts
Teacher's Guide

Years 5 & 6

Peter Clarke

William Collins' dream of knowledge for all began with the publication of his first book in 1819. A self-educated mill worker, he not only enriched millions of lives, but also founded a flourishing publishing house. Today, staying true to this spirit, Collins books are packed with inspiration, innovation and practical expertise. They place you at the centre of a world of possibility and give you exactly what you need to explore it.

Collins. Freedom to teach.

Published by Collins

An imprint of HarperCollins*Publishers*
77 – 85 Fulham Palace Road
Hammersmith
London
W6 8JB

Browse the complete Collins catalogue at
www.collins.co.uk

British Library Cataloguing in Publication Data
A Catalogue record for this publication is available from the British Library

Edited by Gaynor Spry
Cover design by Nikki Kenwood
Cover artwork by Gwyneth Williams
Internal design by Nikki Kenwood
Illustrations by Fran Brylewska and Jouve
Typeset by Jouve

Printed by Martins the Printers Ltd, Berwick upon Tweed

Acknowledgement
The author wishes to thank Brian Molyneaux for his valuable contribution to this publication.

Contents

Introduction

The first aim of The National Curriculum for Mathematics (2014) is to ensure that all pupils:

*'become **fluent** in the fundamentals of mathematics, including through varied and frequent practice with increasingly complex problems over time, so that pupils have conceptual understanding and are able to recall and apply their knowledge rapidly and accurately to problems'.*

Mathematical fluency involves being able to reason mathematically and calculate accurately, efficiently and flexibly.

It is acquired by mastering the following knowledge and skills:

- a thorough conceptual understanding of number, including place value, addition, subtraction, multiplication and division
- the ability to identify patterns and relationships
- the development of strategic approaches to recall and derive number facts.

Essential to mastering these is:

- purposeful dialogue in pairs and as a group
- effective activities to practise and consolidate numerical skills and the recall of number facts
- meaningful and informative assessment, including self-assessment.

Fluency in Number Facts aims to support conceptual understanding, and the development of mental fluency, in basic numerical skills through whole-class, paired and individual games and activities, and assessment.

The series is divided into Key Stage 1 (Years 1 and 2), Lower Key Stage 2 (Years 3 and 4) and Upper Key Stage 2 (Years 5 and 6). It consists of three *Teacher's Guides*, accompanying pupil *Facts and games* books and *CD-ROMs* containing all of the resources needed for the games and activities in downloadable form.

Teacher's Guide

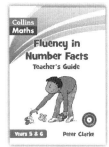

Containing Teacher's Notes on:
- whole-class games and activities
- paired games and activities
- individual activities

Facts and Games book

Containing:
- Maths Facts
- paired games

CD-ROM

Containing:
- Maths Facts from the *Facts and Games* book
- resources for the whole-class games and activities, including PowerPoint slides
- paired games from the *Facts and Games* book as well as additional paired activities
- individual activities
- Mental fluency challenges
- number cards
- assessment and record-keeping formats

Each *Teacher's Guide* and *Facts and Games book* covers three Key domains of becoming fluent in number, and are based on the expectations of The National Curriculum for Mathematics (2014).

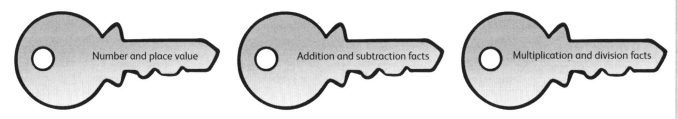

Number and place value

Addition and subtraction facts

Multiplication and division facts

How to use *Fluency in Number Facts*

Fluency in Number Facts is a flexible 'dip in' resource that is designed to be used in many different ways to meet the needs of individual children, and different classroom and school organisational arrangements.

Each of the games and activities is intended to be used for approximately 10 minutes as a way of sharpening children's memory and recall of the basic number facts. Use them either at the start or end of a mathematics lesson or as a quick filler activity at any time throughout the day – a '10 minutes memory maths' session.

The following is a suggested approach to choosing a suitable game or activity:

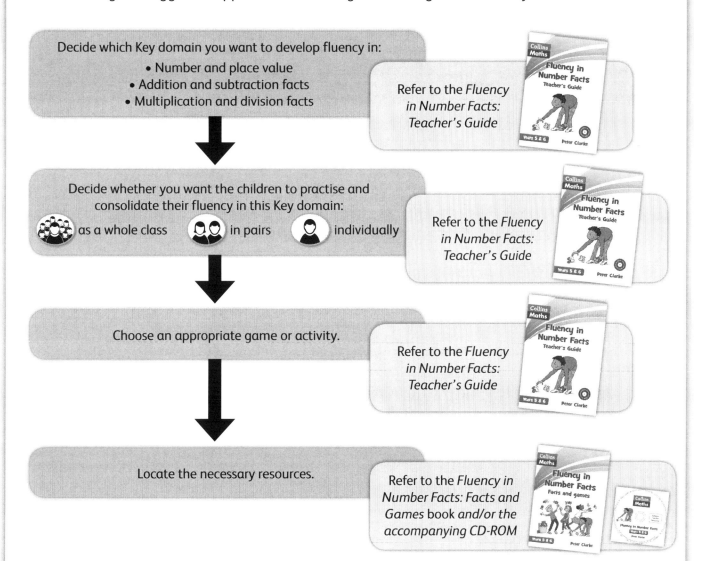

Decide which Key domain you want to develop fluency in:
- Number and place value
- Addition and subtraction facts
- Multiplication and division facts

Refer to the *Fluency in Number Facts: Teacher's Guide*

Decide whether you want the children to practise and consolidate their fluency in this Key domain:

as a whole class   in pairs   individually

Refer to the *Fluency in Number Facts: Teacher's Guide*

Choose an appropriate game or activity.

Refer to the *Fluency in Number Facts: Teacher's Guide*

Locate the necessary resources.

Refer to the *Fluency in Number Facts: Facts and Games* book *and/or* the accompanying CD-ROM

Curriculum information

The games and activities in this pack practise and consolidate the following Upper Key Stage 2 (Years 5 and 6) National Curriculum for Mathematics (2014) Programme of Study:

Year 5

Number and place value

Pupils should be taught to:

- read, write, order and compare numbers to at least 1 000 000 and determine the value of each digit
- count forwards or backwards in steps of powers of 10 for any given number up to 1 000 000
- interpret negative numbers in context, count forwards and backwards with positive and negative whole numbers through zero
- round any number up to 1 000 000 to the nearest 10, 100, 1000, 10 000 and 100 000
- solve number problems and practical problems that involve all of the above

Notes and Guidance (non-statutory)

- [Pupils] should recognise and describe linear number sequences, including those involving fractions and decimals, and find the term-to-term rule.

Addition and subtraction

Pupils should be taught to:

- add and subtract numbers mentally with increasingly large numbers.
- use rounding to check answers to calculations and determine, in the context of a problem, levels of accuracy
- solve addition and subtraction multi-step problems in contexts, deciding which operations and methods to use and why

Notes and Guidance (non-statutory)

- [Pupils] practise mental practise mental calculations with increasingly large numbers to aid fluency.

Multiplication and division

Pupils should be taught to:

- identify multiples and factors, including finding all factor pairs of numbers, and common factors of two numbers
- multiply and divide numbers mentally drawing upon known facts
- multiply and divide whole numbers and those involving decimals by 10, 100 and 1000
- solve problems involving multiplication and division including using their knowledge of factors and multiples, squares and cubes
- solve problems involving multiplication and division, including scaling by simple fractions and problems involving simple rates

Notes and Guidance (non-statutory)

- [Pupils] apply all the multiplication tables and related division facts frequently, commit them to memory and use them confidently to make larger calculations.

Fractions (including decimals and percentages)

Pupils should be taught to:

- round decimals with two decimal places to the nearest whole number and to one decimal place
- read, write, order and compare numbers with up to three decimal places.

Year 6

Number and place value

Pupils should be taught to:

- read, write, order and compare numbers up to 10 000 000 and determine the value of each digit
- round any whole number to a required degree of accuracy
- use negative numbers in context, and calculate intervals across zero
- solve number and practical problems that involve all of the above.

Addition, subtraction, multiplication and division

Pupils should be taught to:

- perform mental calculations, including with mixed operations and large numbers
- identify common factors, common multiples and prime numbers
- solve addition and subtraction multi-step problems in contexts, deciding which operations and methods to use and why
- solve problems involving addition, subtraction, multiplication and division
- use estimation to check answers to calculations and determine, in the context of a problem, levels of accuracy.

Notes and Guidance (non-statutory)

- [Pupils] undertake mental calculations with increasingly large numbers and more complex calculations
- Pupils continue to use all the multiplication tables to calculate mathematical statements in order to maintain their fluency.

Fractions (including decimals and percentages)

Pupils should be taught to:

- identify the value of each digit to three decimal places and multiply and divide numbers by 10, 100 and 1000 where the answers are up to three decimal places
- multiply 1-digit numbers with up to two decimal places by whole numbers.
- solve problems which require answers to be rounded to specified degrees of accuracy

Features of the Fluency in Number Facts: Teacher's Guide

The games and activities in the Fluency in Number Facts: Teacher's Guide are arranged according to the three Key domains. Within each of these Key domains the games and activities are further organised into whole-class, paired or individual games and activities. They are all designed to be used at any time throughout Years 5 & 6.

 ## Whole-class games and activities

This section provides a series of teacher-led games and activities aimed at ensuring the whole class practise and consolidate their fluency in each of the three Key domains.

Each game and activity includes a list of the teacher and pupil resources required as well as instructions and, where appropriate, any variations.

Number and place value

Whole-class games and activities

Say the target number

Objective
- Count forwards or backwards in steps, including those involving decimals and negative numbers

Teacher resources
- none

Pupil resources
- none

What to do
- Arrange the children in a circle.
- Tell the children a start number, for example, 14; a step number, for example, in steps of 7; an end number, for example, 84; a target number between the start and end numbers, for example, 49.
- Children take turns to count round the circle, starting from the start number.
- When a child says the target number, they stand up.
- Children continue the count until the end number is reached.
- The next child to count then goes back to the start number.
- Continue counting in this way until five children are standing.

Variations
- When the end number is said, rather than going back to the start number, the children continue the count backwards from the end number to the start number.
- Play 'Say the target number' counting in multiples of 0·1, 0·2, 0·5 or other decimal steps.
- Play 'Say the target number' involving negative numbers.

18

PowerPoint slides required for some of the whole-class games and activities are located on the accompanying *CD-ROM*.

Whole-class games and activities → PowerPoint slides

PDF files required for some of the whole-class games and activities are located on the accompanying *CD-ROM*.

Whole-class games and activities

Paired games and activities

Games and activities are provided which children undertake in pairs to practise and consolidate their fluency in each of the three Key domains.

Each game and activity includes a list of the resources required as well as instructions and, where appropriate, any variations.

PDF files required for some of the paired games and activities are located on the accompanying *CD-ROM*.

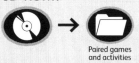

Paired games
and activities

 Multiplication and division facts

Times-table practice — Paired games and activities

Objectives
- Recall and use multiplication facts for multiplication tables up to 12 × 12
- Multiply numbers mentally drawing upon known facts

Pupil resources
- 1–12 dice (per pair)
- 20 counters: 10 counters for each player (per pair)
- container (per pair)

What to do
- Decide which multiplication table you want the children to practice, for example, 8 multiplication table.
- Children take turns to roll the dice.
- Each child multiplies the dice number by 8.
- The first child to call out the correct answer places one of their counters into the container.
- The winner is the first player to place all their counters into the container.

Variations
- Ask the children to multiply the dice number by a multiple of 10 from 20 to 120, i.e. 20 / 30 / 40 / 50 / 60 / 70 / 80 / 90 / 100 / 110 or 120.
- Ask the children to multiply the dice number by a decimal from 0·2 to 1·2, i.e. 0·2 / 0·3 / 0·4 / 0·5 / 0·6 / 0·7 / 0·8 / 0·9 / 1·1 or 1·2.

129

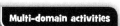 **Multi-domain activities**

Individual activities

Function Machine

Objectives
- Add and subtract numbers mentally with increasingly large numbers and decimals
- Recall and use multiplication and division facts for multiplication tables up to 12 × 12
- Multiply and divide numbers mentally drawing upon known facts
- Multiply and divide whole numbers and those involving decimals by 10, 100 and 1000

Teacher resources
- none

Pupil resources

- 'Function machine' (My Maths Function Machine (B&W or colour version) printed onto card (per child)
- 'Function Machine' strip (per child)

Introduction
Fluency in Number Facts Upper Key Stage 2 includes 36 graded 'Function Machine' strips:

- 18 for Year 5:
- 18 for Year 6:

Each 'Function Machine' strip covers the key addition, subtraction, multiplication and division number facts that children need to be able to recall instantly by the end of Upper Key Stage 2.
Careful consideration has been given to the progression of the Upper Key Stage 2 curriculum, and for each year group the 18 strips have been arranged into three different ability levels, with six strips at each level: **1** easy, **2** average and **3** difficult.
It is recommended that children use the same strip on several consecutive days – perhaps even for a whole week. This way, the majority of children will see themselves making progress, thus providing greater encouragement and self-motivation.

(continued) **175**

 Individual activities

Individual activities are provided which children use, as and when required, to practise and consolidate their fluency in the Key domains of Addition and subtraction, and Multiplication and division.

PDF files required for the individual activities are located on the accompanying *CD-ROM*.

Individual
activities

Features of the *Fluency in Number Facts: Facts and Games* book

Maths Facts

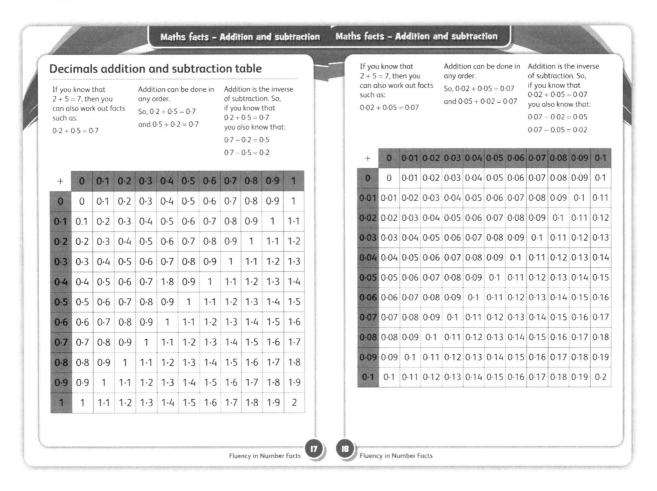

Each *Fluency in Number Facts: Facts and Games* book contains lists of the key addition, subtraction, multiplication and division number facts that children need to be able to recall instantly. These facts are presented in different ways to assist children in developing a deeper understanding, and quick recall, of the facts.

Suggested activities are provided in the *Fluency in Number Facts: Teacher's Guide* which suggests how best to make use of these Maths Facts.

PDF files of the 'Maths Facts' pages from the *Fluency in Number Facts: Facts and Games: Years 5 and 6* book can also be found on the accompanying *CD-ROM*.

Maths facts

 **Paired games**

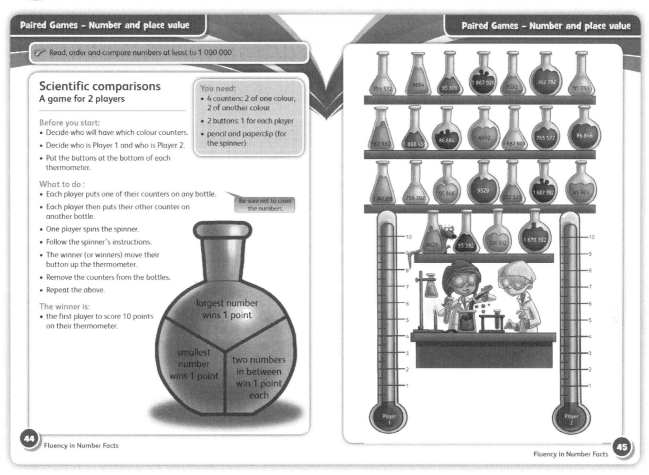

Each *Fluency in Number Facts: Facts and Games* book also includes a bank of paired games to help children become fluent in each of the three Key domains.

The games are organised according to the three Key domains and include a list of the resources required as well as instructions and, where appropriate, any variations.

Additional guidance on how to play the games, along with further variations, can be found in the *Fluency in Number Facts: Teacher's Guide*.

Each game is designed to last approximately ten minutes.

PDF files of the paired games from the *Fluency in Number Facts: Facts and Games: Years 5 and 6* book can also be found on the accompanying *CD-ROM*.

Features of the *Fluency in Number Facts*: *CD-ROM*

The following resources are available to download from the accompanying *CD-ROM*.

Maths Facts

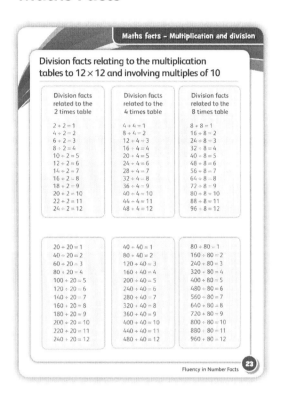

PDF files of the *Fluency in Number Facts: Facts and Games: Years 5 and 6* Maths Facts pages.

 ## Whole-class games and activities

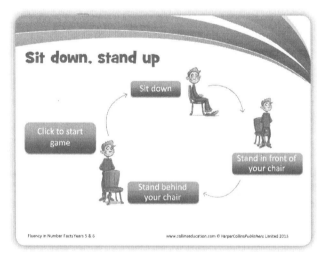

PowerPoint slides required for some of the whole-class games and activities. The slides are also provided as PDF files.

Fluency in Number Facts | Years 5 & 6

Hand me your cards
Teacher's call card for Game 4

• Add and subtract numbers mentally, including multiples of 100 and 1000

What to say	Answer	What to say	Answer
Who has 7317 subtract 5200?	2117	Who has 917 add 1200?	2117
Who has 4761 add 3000?	7761	Who has 7261 add 500?	7761
Who has 400 add 300?	700	Who has 900 subtract 200?	700
Who has 1287 add 4000?	5287	Who has 8287 subtract 3000	5287
Who has 8456 minus 500?	7956	Who has 6156 add 1800?	7956
Who has 200 more than 400?	600	Who has 900 minus 300?	600
Who has 4216 subtract 300?	3916	Who has 2000 more than 1916?	3916
Who has 6200 add 500?	6700	Who has 1000 less than 7700?	6700
Who has 2000 more than 4671?	6671	Who has 3000 less than 9671?	6671
Who has 3845 add 600?	4445	Who has 6745 subtract 2300?	4445
Who has 1300 add 2500?	3800	Who has 5900 subtract 2100?	3800
Who has 8105 minus 3600?	4505	Who has 2805 add 1700?	4505
Who has 7520 add 600?	8120	Who has 8000 add 120?	8120
Who has 400 less than 980?	580	Who has 2580 take away 2000?	580
Who has 4612 subtract 500?	4112	Who has 9112 subtract 5000?	4112
Who has 5310 subtract 400?	4910	Who has 2510 add 2400?	4910
Who has 1200 add 5300?	6500	Who has 7200 minus 700?	6500
Who has 3000 add 4000?	7000	Who has 5000 add 2000?	7000

Easier question
More difficult question

www.collinseducation.com © HarperCollinsPublishers Limited 2013

PDF files required for some of the whole-class games and activities.

Paired games and activities

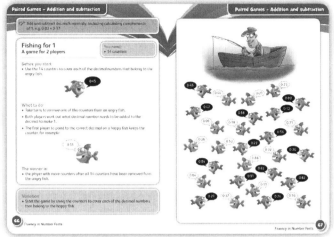

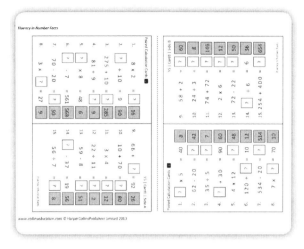

PDF files of the *Fluency in Number Facts: Facts and Games: Years 5 and 6* paired games.

PDF files required for some of the paired games and activities.

 ### Individual activities

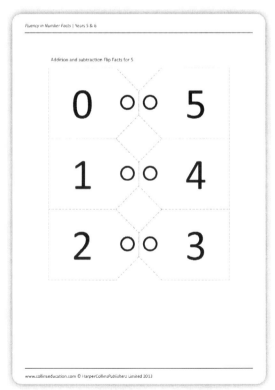

PDF files required for some of the individual activities.

Written activities

Refer to pages 146–169 of the *Fluency in Number Facts: Teacher's Guide: Years 5 and 6* for an explanation as to how to use each of the written activities.

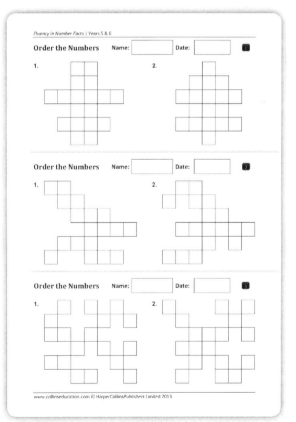

WORD files required for the written activities.

Mental fluency challenges

Fluency in Number Facts includes 36 graded Mental fluency challenges (18 for Year 5, and 18 for Year 6).

These challenges are aimed at providing children with further practice and consolidation and also at offering teachers a means of assessing individual children's proficiency in the mental recall of number facts.

Each challenge covers the key addition, subtraction, multiplication and division number facts that children need to be able to recall instantly by the end of Upper Key Stage 2.

Careful consideration has been given to the progression of the Upper Key Stage 2 curriculum, and for each year group the 18 challenges have been arranged into three different ability levels, with six exercises at each level: easy **Challenge 1**, average **Challenge 2** and challenging **Challenge 3**.

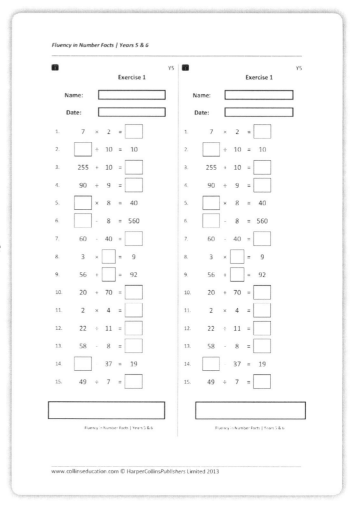

It is recommended that children do the same exercise on two or three consecutive days. This way, the majority of children will see themselves making progress over the two or three days, thus providing greater encouragement and self-motivation.

It is envisaged that these exercises could be given to the children either where they take as long as they need to answer all ten questions, or as a timed exercise (for example: *I want you to answer as many of these questions as you can in eight minutes. Ready? Go!*). Alternatively, to encourage speed and recall, set the children to work and as they finish the exercise they raise their hand and you tell them how long it took them to complete it.

Both PDF and WORD versions of the Mental fluency exercises are provided.

The WORD version is provided so that individual schools or classes can, if they perceive it necessary, modify the content of the challenges to better suit the needs of their children. However, it is important to be aware that if changes are made to the content, that the continuity and progression of the challenges will be affected.

As well as the WORD and PDF versions of the 'Mental fluency challenges', there is also an audio file of each exercise.

A 'Mental fluency challenge answer sheet' is also provided for children to use to record their answers when using the auditory version of the challenges.

Refer to pages 170–172 of the *Fluency in Number Facts: Teacher's Guide: Years 5 and 6* for a more detailed explanation as to how to use the 'Mental fluency challenges'.

Number cards

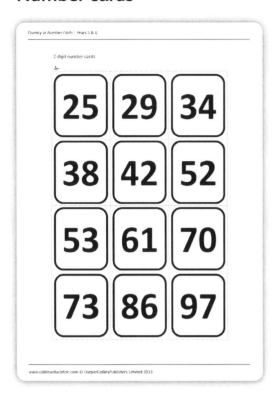

PDF files of the number cards required for some of the games and activities.

Assessment and record-keeping formats

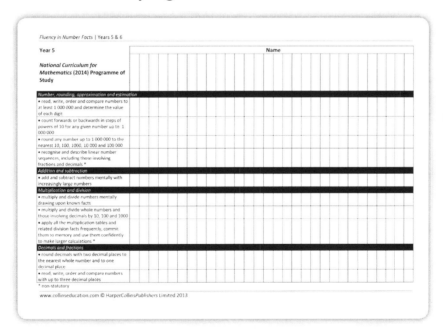

WORD files are provided for each of the following assessment and record-keeping formats:

- Record of Pupil Progress
  - Year 5
  - Year 6

These charts are designed to enable teachers to keep a record of the level of mastery that individual children have achieved in the Number and place value; Addition and subtraction; and Multiplication and division National Curriculum for Mathematics (2014) Programmes of Study. The assessment criteria provided on each chart can be modified to better suit the requirements of individual schools and classes.

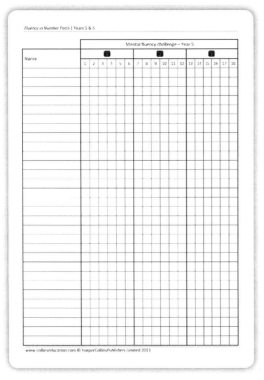

- Record of Mental fluency challenges:
  - Year 5
  - Year 6

- Record of Function machine strips:
  - Year 5
  - Year 6

- Record of Paired calculations cards:
  - Year 5
  - Year 6

These charts are designed to enable teachers to keep a record of which activity individual children have completed.

Record of Mental fluency challenges can also be used to record children's scores.

- Pupil self-assessment booklet:
  - Year 5
  - Year 6

These booklets are designed to be completed by individual children at the end of each term to assist them in gauging their own level of proficiency in each of the three Key domains. The assessment criteria provided on each booklet can be modified to better suit the requirements of individual classes and children. Also make sure that you print the Word files as a booklet as shown.

CD-ROM **flowchart**

The flowchart below has been included to assist teachers in locating the resources found on the accompanying *Fluency in Number Facts: CD-ROM*.

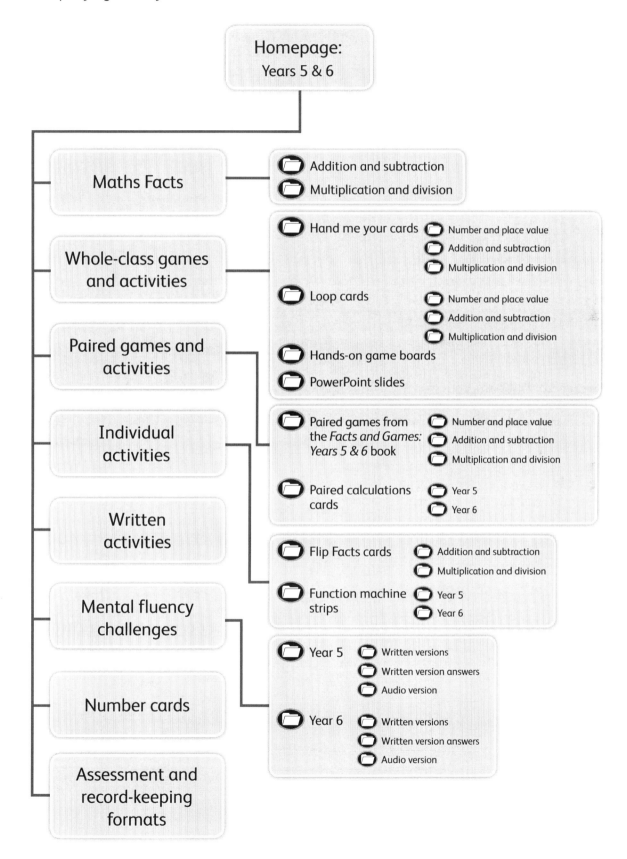

Say the target number

Objective

- Count forwards or backwards in steps, including those involving decimals and negative numbers

Teacher resources

- none

Pupil resources

- none

What to do

- Arrange the children in a circle.
- Tell the children a start number, for example, 14; a step number, for example, in steps of 7; an end number, for example, 84; a target number between the start and end numbers, for example, 49.
- Children take turns to count round the circle, starting from the start number.
- When a child says the target number, they stand up.
- Children continue the count until the end number is reached.
- The next child to count then goes back to the start number.
- Continue counting in this way until five children are standing.

Variations

- When the end number is said, rather than going back to the start number, the children continue the count backwards from the end number to the start number.
- Play 'Say the target number' counting in multiples of 0·1, 0·2, 0·5 or other decimal steps.
- Play 'Say the target number' involving negative numbers.

And the winner is...

Objective

- Count forwards or backwards in steps, including those involving decimals, negative numbers

Teacher resources

Whole-class games and activities → PowerPoint slides

- 'And the winner is…'

Pupil resources

- none

And the winner is

Starting from 64

Count on in steps of 1

The winner says 115

Fluency in Number Facts Years 5 & 6   www.collinseducation.com © HarperCollinsPublishers Limited 2013

What to do

- Arrange the children into pairs.
- Display one of the 'And the winner is…' slides.
- Demonstrate with a child how to play the game:
  - decide who will start the count at the 'Starting from…' number, for example, 'Starting from 64'
  - take turns to count in the steps shown, for example, 'Count on in steps of 1'
  - the winner is the player that says the winning number, i.e. 115.
- Children play the games in pairs.
- Before they begin each game, encourage the children to predict who will be the winner.
- Use other 'And the winner is…' slides, to play several rounds.

Variation

- Change the start number, step and winning number on the slides.

Counting stick

Objective

- Count forwards or backwards in steps, including those involving decimals and negative numbers

Teacher resources

- counting stick, i.e. a stick ideally 1 metre in length, marked off in ten equal divisions. If possible, add pieces of Velcro at each divider in order to attach labels to the stick.

- small labels showing numbers 0–10, multiples of 2, 3, 4, 5, 6, 7, 8, 9, 10, 11, 12, 25, 50, 100 and 1000 to the 10th multiple (if appropriate). Alternatively, use Post-it Notes for the labels.

Pupil resources

- none

What to do

- Decide which multiples you want the children to practise, i.e. count in multiples of 7 from any number, forwards or backwards.
- Name one end of the stick 0 and the other 70. Count in steps of 7 forwards and when confident, backwards.
- Randomly point to divisions and ask questions such as: *Which number belongs here?* If appropriate, stick the corresponding label on the stick.
- When confident, name one end of the stick a number other than 0, for example, 14. Children count on from this number.

Variations

- Count in multiples of 2, 3, 4, 5, 6, 7, 8, 9, 10, 11, 12, 25, 50, 100 or 1000 from any number, forwards or backwards. Name one end of the stick 0 and the other end the 10th multiple. When confident, name one end of the stick a multiple other than 0.
- Use the counting stick to count in multiples of 0·1, 0·2, 0·5 or other decimal steps.
- Include negative numbers.

Fizz / Fizz Buzz

Objective

- Count forwards or backwards in steps, including those involving decimals and negative numbers

Teacher resources

- none

Pupil resources

- none

What to do

- Decide which multiples you want the children to practise, e.g. multiples of 7.
- Recite the multiples of 7, from 7 to 84 with the class, i.e. 7, 14, 21, 28…
- Ask the children to stand.
- Count forwards round the class in steps of 1, from 1 to at least 84.
- When a multiple of 7 is reached instead of saying the number the child says *Fizz*. i.e. 1st child says *1*, 2nd child says *2*…, 6th child says *6*, 7th child says *Fizz*, 8th child says *8*… 14th child says *Fizz*…
- Continue counting round the class for as long as is appropriate.

Variations

- Play 'Fizz' for the multiples of 2, 4, 5, 6, 7, 8, 9, 10, 11 or 12 counting forwards to the 12th multiple.
- Play 'Fizz' for the multiples of 2, 3, 4, 5, 6, 7, 8, 9, 10, 11 or 12 counting backwards from the 12th multiple.
- Play 'Fizz' counting in multiples of 0·1, 0·2, 0·5 or other decimal steps.
- Play 'Fizz' involving negative numbers.
- Play 'Fizz Buzz'. For example, for any multiple of 7 say *Fizz* and for any multiple of 8 say *Buzz*. If the number is a multiple of both 7 and 8, for example, 56, say *Fizz Buzz*.

Say it and you're out

Objective

- Count forwards or backwards in steps, including those involving decimals and negative numbers

Teacher resources

- none

Pupil resources

- none

What to do

- Decide which multiples you want the children to practise, e.g. multiples of 7.
- Recite the multiples of 7 from 7 to 84 with the class, i.e. 7, 14, 21, 28…
- Write any three of these multiples of 7 on the board, for example, 21, 42 and 77.
- Ask the children to stand.
- Count forwards round the class reciting the multiples of 7 from 7 to 84, i.e. 1st child says 7, 2nd child says 14, 3rd child says 21… (the 13th child starts from 7 again).
- When a child says one of the multiples of 7 written on the board, that child has to sit down and is out.
- Continue counting round the class until one child is left standing. This child is the winner.

Variations

- Count forwards and backwards round the class reciting the multiples of 7 from 7 to 84, i.e. 1st child says 7, 2nd child says 14, 3rd child says 21… 12th child says 84, 13th child says 77, 14th child says 70…
- When there are only four or five children left standing, ask the rest of the class if they can work out who will be the winner.
- Play 'Say it and you're out' counting in multiples of 1, 2, 3, 5, 6, 7, 8, 9, 10, 11, 12, 25, 50, 100 or 1000.
- Play 'Say it and you're out' counting in multiples of 0·1, 0·2, 0·5 or other decimal steps.
- Play 'Say it and you're out' involving negative numbers.

Remember the numbers

Objectives

- Read, order and compare numbers and determine the value of each digit
- Round any whole number to a required degree of accuracy
- Read, order and compare numbers with up to three decimal places
- Identify the value of each digit to three decimal places
- Round decimals with two decimal places to the nearest whole number and to one decimal place
- Multiply and divide whole numbers and those involving decimals by 10, 100 and 1000

Teacher resources

Whole-class games and activities → PowerPoint slides

- 'Remember the numbers'

Pupil resources

- none

Remember the numbers

8·5   9·4

3·6   4·2

Fluency in Number Facts Years 5 & 6   www.collinseducation.com © HarperCollinsPublishers Limited 2013

What to do

- Say: *I'm going to show you a slide with some numbers on it. I'm then going to hide the numbers and ask you some questions about them. You need to try and remember the numbers before I hide them. Ready?*
- Display one of the 'Remember the numbers' slides for about ten seconds.
- Hide the slide, pause, then ask questions similar to the following:
  - *What is the largest (smallest) number?*
  - *Which number has 5 tenths?*
  - *Which number has 3 ones (units)?*
  - *Which numbers are less than (greater than) 5?*
  - *Which numbers round to 4?*
  - *Which number is the answer to 94 divided by 10?*

Variations

- Repeat using other 'Remember the numbers' slides.
- Change the numbers on the 'Remember the numbers' slides.

Point to it

Objectives

- Read, write, order and compare numbers up to 1 000 000 and determine the value of each digit
- Read, write, order and compare numbers with up to three decimal places
- Identify the value of each digit to three decimal places

Teacher resources

Whole-class games and activities → PowerPoint slides

- 'Point to it'

Pupil resources

- pencil and paper (per child)

Point to it

1000	2000	3000	4000	5000	6000	7000	8000	9000
100	200	300	400	500	600	700	800	900
10	20	30	40	50	60	70	80	90
1	2	3	4	5	6	7	8	9

Fluency in Number Facts Years 5 & 6   www.collinseducation.com © HarperCollinsPublishers Limited 2013

What to do

- Decide which range of numbers you want the children to use and choose the appropriate slide.
- If using the second slide for example, ask each child to write down three 4-digit numbers, for example, 4756, 1283, 3859.
- Display the second slide and point to a number on the slide for example, 800.
- If a child has a number with the same place value, they cross it out, i.e. 3859.
- If they don't, they do nothing.
- The winner is the first child to cross out all 12 digits in their three numbers.

(**Note:** Be sure to keep a record of the numbers pointed to for checking purposes.)

Variations

- Display the first slide and ask each child to write down three 3-digit numbers, for example, 521, 657, 279.
- Display the third slide and ask each child to write down two 5-digit numbers, for example, 46 319, 83 495.
- Display the fourth slide and ask each child to write down two 6-digit numbers, for example, 847 238, 413 192.
- Display the fifth slide and ask each child to write down three decimal numbers, each with three digits, to one decimal place, for example, 53·4, 36·9, 17·2.
- Display the sixth slide and ask each child to write down three decimal numbers, each with three digits, to two decimal places, for example, 7·28, 8·39, 2·54.
- Display the seventh slide and ask each child to write down three decimal numbers, each with four digits, to three decimal places, for example, 5·184, 3·753, 6·462.

Guess the number

Objectives

- Read, order and compare numbers up to 10 000 000 and determine the value of each digit
- Round any whole number to a required degree of accuracy
- Read, order and compare numbers with up to three decimal places
- Identify the value of each digit to three decimal places
- Round decimals with two decimal places to the nearest whole number and to one decimal place

Teacher resources

- small pieces of paper or card
- hat
- something to fasten the paper or card onto the hat (for example, a paperclip)

Pupil resources

- none

What to do

- Write a whole number on a small piece of paper or card, for example, 384 000, and fasten it to the hat.
- Ask a child to come to the front and, keeping the number a secret from this child, put the hat on them.
- Depending on the number you choose, you may wish to give the children one or two clues, for example: *It is a multiple of 1000.*
- This child then asks questions to the rest of the class to find out the number on the hat. However, s/he can only ask questions that will give a 'yes' or 'no' response, for example: *Is it a 4-digit number? Is it a 6-digit number? Is it less than 500 000?*
- Repeat using different numbers with other children.
- Who can guess the secret number asking the fewest questions?

Variation

- Write a decimal number on a small piece of paper or card.

Place value bingo

Objectives

- Read, write, order and compare numbers up to 1 000 000 and determine the value of each digit
- Read, write, order and compare numbers with up to three decimal places
- Identify the value of each digit to three decimal places

Teacher resources

Whole-class games and activities → PowerPoint slides

- 'Bingo'

Pupil resources

- pencil and paper or small individual whiteboard and pen (per child)

Bingo
Hundredths

3·67	5·51	7·83	8·19	2·67	9·57
6·28	1·26	4·54	0·45	5·92	3·98
0·19	2·42	6·96	7·63	4·39	1·84
8·25	3·23	1·31	9·96	0·53	4·19
2·71	6·35	7·58	5·42	8·78	9·86
5·62	3·74	8·47	4·84	7·31	6·75

Fluency in Number Facts Years 5 & 6   www.collinseducation.com © HarperCollinsPublishers Limited 2013

What to do

- Decide which range of numbers you want the children to use and choose the appropriate slide.
- Ask each child to write down any five numbers from the slide.
- If using the 'Bingo: Hundredths' slide for example, say statements similar to the following:
  - *Cross out any number that has 4 tenths.*
  - *Cross out any number that has 3 ones.*
  - *Cross out any number that has 8 hundredths.*
  - *Cross out the number that has 8 ones, 2 tenths and 5 hundredths.*
  - *Cross out the number that has 8 tenths, 7 ones and 3 hundredths.*
- Children see if any of their five numbers match the description.
- If a child has a match, they cross out that number.
- The winner is the first child to cross out all five of their numbers and call out 'Bingo!'

(**Note:** Be sure to keep a record of the numbers for checking purposes.)

Variations

- Ask the children to write down more or fewer than five numbers from the slide.
- Use the 'Bingo: 2-digit numbers', 'Bingo: 3-digit numbers', 'Bingo: 4-digit numbers', 'Bingo: 5-digit numbers', 'Bingo: 6-digit numbers', 'Bingo: Tenths' and 'Bingo: Thousandths' slides.

Higher or lower?

Objectives

- Count forwards or backwards in steps, including those involving decimals
- Read, order and compare numbers up to 10 000 000 and determine the value of each digit
- Read, order and compare numbers with up to three decimal places
- Identify the value of each digit to three decimal places

Teacher resources

Higher or lower Four-digit numbers

Higher   Lower

4847

Whole-class games and activities → PowerPoint slides

- 'Higher or lower'

Pupil resources

- none

What to do

- Decide which range of numbers you want the children to use and choose the appropriate set of slides.
- Display the first slide. If using the 'Higher or Lower: 4-digit numbers' for example, the number 4847.
- Tell the children that there are ten slides altogether, and that each slide has a 4-digit number on it.
- Ask the children to decide whether they think the next number will be higher or lower than the current number, i.e. 4847.
- If they think the number is going to be larger, they put their hands in the air.
- If they think the number is going to be smaller, they put their hands on their head.
- Display the second slide, i.e. 7526.
- Keep going until all ten slides are revealed.

(**Note:** The question mark at the side of the second to last slide is to indicate that the next slide is the last slide.)

Variations

- Use the 'Higher or lower: 2-digit numbers', 'Higher or lower: 3-digit numbers', 'Higher or lower: 5-digit numbers', 'Higher or lower: 6-digit numbers' and 'Higher or lower: 1–10 millions' set of slides. Tell the children that there are ten slides altogether.
- Use the 'Higher or lower: Tenths' set of slides. Tell the children that there are 11 slides in the range 1 to 2.
- Use the 'Higher or lower: Hundredths' set of slides. Tell the children that there are 11 slides in the range 1·1 to 1·2.
- Use the 'Higher or lower: Thousandths' set of slides. Tell the children that there are 11 slides in the range 1·01 to 1·02.
- Use the 'Higher or lower: Multiples of…' set of slides. Tell the children that there are 12 slides. The default version is set for multiples of 6. However these can be changed to include the 12 multiples of any multiplication table up to 12 × 12.
- Re-arrange the order of the slides. Ensure that the second to last slide has the question mark on it and that the last slide has a 'glow' around the number.
- Change the numbers on the slide.

Gladiators

Objectives

- Count forwards or backwards in steps, including those involving decimals
- Read, order and compare numbers up to 10 000 000 and determine the value of each digit
- Round any whole number to a required degree of accuracy
- Read, order and compare numbers with up to three decimal places
- Identify the value of each digit to three decimal places
- Round decimals with two decimal places to the nearest whole number and to one decimal place
- Multiply and divide whole numbers and those involving decimals by 10, 100 and 1000

Teacher resources

Whole-class games and activities → PowerPoint slides

- 'Gladiators'

Pupil resources

- 2 × rulers or 'swords'

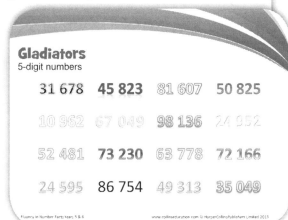

Gladiators
5-digit numbers

31 678	45 823	81 607	50 825
10 962	67 049	98 136	24 952
52 481	73 230	63 778	72 166
24 595	86 754	49 313	35 049

Fluency in Number Facts Years 5 & 6   www.collinseducation.com © HarperCollinsPublishers Limited 2013

What to do

- Decide which range of numbers you want the children to use.
- Display the appropriate slide.
- Ask two children to stand either side of the numbers.
- If using the 'Gladiators: 5-digit numbers' slide for example, say statements similar to the following:
  - *Point to the number 98 136.*
  - *Point to the number that has 7 ten thousands, 3 thousands, 2 hundreds, 3 tens and 0 units.*
  - *Point to the number that has 2 tens, 3 ones and 8 hundreds, 4 ten thousands and 5 thousands.*
  - *Point to any number greater than 65 000.*
  - *Point to any even number between 50 000 and 90 000.*
  - *Point to the number that is 10 times 7323.*
  - *Point to a number that rounds to 70 000.*
- The first child to point to the correct number stays in. The other child sits down.
- Quickly choose another child to come and take the place of the child that just sat down.
- Continue as above.
- Which child can stay in the longest?

Variations

- The children sitting down ask the two children standing by the numbers a question where the answer is on the slide.
- To quicken the game, have two children standing either side of the numbers, one behind the other. When a child loses and has to sit down, there is an immediate replacement.

Gladiators

(continued)

- Use the 'Gladiators: Numbers 1–20', 'Gladiators: 2-digit numbers', 'Gladiators: 3-digit numbers', 'Gladiators: 4-digit numbers', 'Gladiators: 6-digit numbers' or 'Gladiators: Millions' slides.
- Use the 'Gladiators: 2 times table' slide. Say statements similar to the following:
  - *Point to the next number in this pattern: 6, 8, 10, 12.*
  - *Point to the next number in this pattern: 24, 22, 20, 18.*
- Use the following slides in a similar way: 'Gladiators: 3 / 4 / 5 / 6 / 7 / 8 / 9 / 10 / 11 / 12 times table'.
- Use the 'Gladiators: Multiples of 20' slide. Say statements similar to the following:
  - *Point to the next number in this pattern: 40, 60, 80, 100.*
  - *Point to the next number in this pattern: 200, 180, 160, 140.*
- Use the following slides in a similar way: 'Gladiators: Multiples of 30 / 40 / 50 / 60 / 70 / 80 / 90 / 100 / 110 / 120'.
- Use the 'Gladiators: Multiples of 0.2' slide. Say statements similar to the following:
  - *Point to the next number in this pattern: 0·6, 0·8, 1, 1·2.*
  - *Point to the next number in this pattern: 1·6, 1·4, 1·2, 0·8.*
- Use the following slides in a similar way: 'Gladiators: Multiples of 0·3 / 0·4 / 0·5 / 0·6 / 0·7 / 0·8 / 0·9 / 1·1 / 1·2.
- To consolidate children's understanding use the 'Gladiators: 2, 5 and 10 times tables' slide, say statements similar to the following:
  - *Point to the next number in this pattern: 10, 15, 20, 25.*
  - *Point to the next number in this pattern: 24, 22, 20, 18.*
  - *Point to the next number in this pattern: 30, 40, 50, 60.*
- Use the following slides in a similar way: 'Gladiators: 3, 4 and 8 times tables' and 'Gladiators: 6, 7, 9, 11 and 12 times tables'.
- To reinforce the relationship between different multiplication tables use 'Gladiators: 2, 4 and 8 times tables' and 'Gladiators: 3, 6 and 12 times tables'.
- To practise and consolidate rounding to the nearest 10, 100 or 1000 use the 'Gladiators: Multiples of 10 and 100' and 'Gladiators: Multiples of 100 and 1000' slide. Ask questions similar to the following:
  - *What is 43 rounded to the nearest multiple of 10?*
  - *What is 271 rounded to the nearest multiple of 100?*
  - *What is 6467 rounded to the nearest multiple of 1000?*
- To practise place value, comparing, ordering and rounding decimals use the 'Gladiators: Tenths', 'Gladiators: Hundredths' and 'Gladiators: Thousandths' slides. Say statements similar to the following:
  - *Point to the number that has 3 hundredths.*
  - *Point to the number that has 7 thousandths.*
  - *Point to the number that is between 7·9 and 8·7.*
  - *Point to the number that is between 3·25 and 4·75.*
  - *Point to a number that rounds to 4.*
  - *Point to the number that rounds to 6·4.*
  - *What is 42 divided by 10?*
  - *What is 196 divided by 100?*

Hands-on

Objectives

- Count forwards or backwards in steps, including those involving decimals
- Read, order and compare numbers up to 10 000 000 and determine the value of each digit
- Round any whole number to a required degree of accuracy
- Read, order and compare numbers with up to three decimal places
- Identify the value of each digit to three decimal places
- Round decimals with two decimal places to the nearest whole number and to one decimal place
- Multiply and divide whole numbers and those involving decimals by 10, 100 and 1000

Teacher resources

- none

Pupil resources

Whole-class games and activities → Hands-on game boards

- 'Hands-on' game board (per pair)

What to do

- Decide which range of numbers you want the children to use.
- Arrange the children into pairs and provide each pair with a copy of the appropriate 'Hands-on' game board.
- Tell the children to put the game board between them and each child to put their index finger on a hand at the bottom of the game board.
- If using the 'Hands-on: 5-digit numbers' game board for example, say statements similar to the following:
  - *Point to the number 28 569.*
  - *Point to any number larger than 45 000.*
  - *Point to the number between 29 957 and 32 573.*
  - *Point to the number that is 1 more than 57 189*
  - *Point to the number that is 10 more than 61 692.*
  - *Point to the number that is 100 less than 14 135.*
  - *Point to the number that has 3 tens of thousands, 2 thousands, 6 hundreds, 5 tens and 9 units.*
  - *Point to the number that has 3 units, 1 ten, 8 hundreds, 2 tens of thousands and 9 thousands.*
  - *Point to any number that rounds to 60 000.*
- The first child to point to the correct number wins.
- Children keep count of how many rounds they win.
- Play for as long as is appropriate.
- The winner in each pair is the child who wins more rounds.

Variations

- Provide each pair with a pile of counters. As a child wins a game they take a counter. The winner in each pair is the child who wins more counters.

Hands-on

(continued)

- Use the 'Hands-on: Numbers 1–20', 'Hands-on: 2-digit numbers', 'Hands-on: 3-digit numbers', 'Hands-on: 4-digit numbers', 'Hands-on: 6-digit numbers' and 'Hands-on: 1–10 million' game boards.

- Use the 'Hands-on: Multiples of 2' game board. Say statements similar to the following:
  - *Point to the next number in this pattern: 8, 10, 12, 14.*
  - *Point to the next number in this pattern: 24, 22, 20, 18.*

- Use the following 'Hands-on' game boards in a similar way: 'Hands-on: Multiples of 3 / 4 / 5 / 6 / 7 / 8 / 9 / 10 / 11 / 12' game boards.

- Use the 'Hands-on: Multiples of 20' game board. Say statements similar to the following:
  - *Point to the next number in this pattern: 60, 80, 100, 120.*
  - *Point to the next number in this pattern: 180, 160, 140, 120.*

- Use the following 'Hands-on' game boards in a similar way: 'Hands-on: Multiples of 30 / 40 / 50 / 60 / 70 / 80 / 90 / 100 / 110 / 120' game boards.

- Use the 'Hands-on: Multiples of 0.2' game board. Say statements similar to the following:
  - *Point to the next number in this pattern: 0·8, 1, 1·2, 1·4.*
  - *Point to the next number in this pattern: 1·8, 1·6, 1·4, 1·2.*

- Use the following 'Hands-on' game boards in a similar way: 'Hands-on: Multiples of 0·3 / 0·4 / 0·5 / 0·6 / 0·7 / 0·8 / 0·9 / 1·1 / 1·2' game boards.

- To practise and consolidate rounding to the nearest 10, 100 or 1000 use the 'Hands-on: Multiples of 10 and 100' game board and 'Hands-on: Multiples of 100 and 1000' game board. Ask questions similar to the following:
  - *What is 83 rounded to the nearest multiple of 10?*
  - *What is 786 rounded to the nearest multiple of 100?*
  - *What is 5348 rounded to the nearest multiple of 1000?*

- To practise place value, comparing, ordering and rounding decimals, use the 'Hands-on: Tenths' game board, 'Hands-on: Hundredths' game board and 'Hands-on: Thousandths' game board. Say statements similar to the following:
  - *Point to the decimal number 2·4.*
  - *Point to any decimal number larger than 5·5.*
  - *Point to the number between 2·9 and 4·2.*
  - *Point to any decimal with 6 tenths.*
  - *Point to a number that rounds to 6.*
  - *Point to the number that rounds to 3·3.*
  - *What is 49 divided by 10?*
  - *What is 239 divided by 100?*

Who's left standing?

Objectives

- Read, order and compare numbers up to 1 000 000 and determine the value of each digit
- Read, order and compare numbers with up to three decimal places
- Identify the value of each digit to three decimal places

Teacher resources

- none

Pupil resources

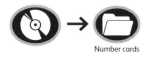

Number cards

- '3-digit number cards', '4-digit number cards', '5-digit number cards', '6-digit number cards', Tenths number cards', 'Hundredths number cards' or 'Thousandths number cards' (one card per child)

What to do

Game 1: Order and compare 3-digit numbers

- Provide each child with a '3-digit number card'. (**Note:** Ensure you use the 12 '3-digit number cards' provided on the CD-ROM.)

Say: *Everyone stand up. Look at the number on your card. Sit down if the number on your card is:*

- *between 489 and 548 (504)*
- *between 762 and 868 (860)*
- *between 310 and 411 (318)*
- *between 591 and 674 (647)*
- *less than 200 (193)*
- *between 661 and 728 (683)*

- *between 362 and 467 (429)*
- *between 901 and 1001 (936)*
- *between 699 and 799 (735)*
- *between 539 and 584 (568)*
- *between 250 and 300 (255)*

The winners are the children still standing with 471 on their cards.

Game 2: Order and compare 4-digit numbers

- Provide each child with a 4-digit number card. (**Note:** Ensure you use the 12 '4-digit number cards' provided on the CD-ROM.)
- Say: *Everyone stand up. Look at the number on your card. Sit down if the number on your card is:*

- *between 5207 and 5935 (5463)*
- *between 1856 and 3198 (2518)*
- *between 8183 and 8674 (8256)*
- *between 3561 and 4367 (4071)*
- *between 6901 and 8201 (7942)*
- *between 4289 and 5037 (4695)*

- *between 5583 and 6539 (6324)*
- *less than 1850 (1783)*
- *between 2846 and 3725 (3270)*
- *between 8563 and 9574 (9036)*
- *between 4836 and 5381 (5189)*

The winners are the children still standing with 6857 on their cards.

Who's left standing?

(continued)

Game 3: Order and compare 5-digit numbers

- Provide each child with a '5-digit number card'. (**Note:** Ensure you use the 12 '5-digit number cards' provided on the CD-ROM.)
- Say: *Everyone stand up. Look at the number on your card. Sit down if the number on your card is:*
  - *between 53 247 and 62 935 (62 098)*
  - *between 42 053 and 49 471 (47 326)*
  - *between 68 376 and 75 367 (74 841)*
  - *between 28 598 and 40 000 (39 513)*
  - *between 86 103 and 94 738 (91 026)*
  - *between 16 498 and 24 841 (18 267)*
  - *between 77 456 and 87 354 (83 284)*
  - *between 48 016 and 57 219 (51 634)*
  - *between 39 745 and 45 524 (40 175)*
  - *between 62 980 and 71 376 (63 750)*
  - *between 19 487 and 36 389 (26 409)*

The winners are the children still standing with 75 982 on their cards.

Game 4: Order and compare 6-digit numbers

- Provide each child with a '6-digit number card'. (**Note:** Ensure you use the 12 '6-digit number cards' provided on the CD-ROM.)
- Say: *Everyone stand up. Look at the number on your card. Sit down if the number on your card is:*
  - *between 461 282 and 537 146 (495 326)*
  - *between 763 987 and 881 465 (849 362)*
  - *between 116 387 and 153 498 (138 409)*
  - *between 608 957 and 714 873 (619 832)*
  - *between 193 679 and 263 571 (256 193)*
  - *between 665 371 and 835 481 (720 950)*
  - *between 158 376 and 234 058 (173 584)*
  - *between 534 871 and 592 736 (542 678)*
  - *more than 859 346 (950 173)*
  - *between 553 876 and 611 472 (604 751)*
  - *between 284 525 and 452 856 (381 247)*

The winners are the children still standing with 267 015 on their cards.

Game 5: Recognise the place value of each digit in a 3-digit number

- Provide each child with a '3-digit number card'. (**Note:** Ensure you use the 12 '3-digit number cards' provided on the CD-ROM.)
- Say: *Everyone stand up. Look at the number on your card. Sit down if the number on your card has:*
  - *5 tens (255)*
  - *1 hundred (193)*
  - *6 ones (or units) (936)*
  - *7 ones (or units) (647)*
  - *7 tens (471)*
  - *9 ones (or units) (429)*
  - *8 tens (683)*
  - *8 hundreds (860)*
  - *1 ten (318)*
  - *7 hundreds (735)*
  - *4 ones (or units) (504)*

The winners are the children still standing with 568 on their cards.

(*continued*)

Number and place value

Who's left standing?

(continued)

Game 6: Recognise the place value of each digit in a 4-digit number

- Provide each child with a '4-digit number card'. (**Note:** Ensure you use the 12 '4-digit number cards' provided on the CD-ROM.)
- Say: *Everyone stand up. Look at the number on your card. Sit down if the number on your card has:*
  - *7 ones (or units) (6857)*   *– 4 tens (7942)*   *– 9 tens (4695)*
  - *7 hundreds (1783)*   *– 3 thousands (3270)*   *– 8 thousands (8256)*
  - *9 thousands (9036)*   *– 8 ones (or units) (2518)* *– 1 hundred (5189)*
  - *1 one (or unit) (4071)*   *– 3 hundreds (6324)*

The winners are the children still standing with 5463 on their cards.

Game 7: Recognise the place value of each digit in a 5-digit number

- *Provide each child with a '5-digit number card'.* (**Note:** Ensure you use the 12 '5-digit number cards' provided on the CD-ROM.)
- *Say: Everyone stand up. Look at the number on your card. Sit down if the number on your card has:*
  - *9 thousands (39 513)*   *– 2 ones (or units) (75 982)*   *– 4 hundreds (26 409)*
  - *8 hundreds (74 841)*   *– 8 ten thousands (83 284)*   *– 3 tens (51 634)*
  - *5 tens (63 750)*   *– 7 ones (or units) (18 267)*   *– 2 thousands (62 098)*
  - *3 hundreds (47 326)*   *– 9 ten thousands (91 026)*

The winners are the children still standing with 40 175 on their cards.

Game 8: Recognise the place value of each digit in a 6-digit number

- Provide each child with a '6-digit number card'. (**Note:** Ensure you use the 12 '6-digit number cards' provided on the CD-ROM.)
- Say: *Everyone stand up. Look at the number on your card. Sit down if the number on your card has:*
  - *4 tens (381 247)*   *– 9 ten thousands (495 326)*   *– 6 tens (849 362)*
  - *5 hundreds (173 584)*   *– 6 thousands (256 193)*   *– 3 ten thousands (138 409)*
  - *9 hundred thousands*   *– 7 hundred thousands*   *– 8 hundreds (619 832)*
    (950 173)   *(720 950)*
  - *5 ones (or units) (267 015)* *– 2 thousands (542 678)*

The winners are the children still standing with 604 751 on their cards.

Game 9: Compare numbers with one decimal place
     Recognise the place value of each digit in a number with one decimal place

- Provide each child with a 'Tenths number card'. (**Note:** Ensure you use the 12 'Tenths number cards' provided on the CD-ROM.)
- Say: *Everyone stand up. Look at the number on your card. Sit down if the number on your card:*
  - *is between 5·2 and 5·9 (5·6)* *– is between 1 and 1·5 (1·2)*   *– is between 7·5 and 8·4 (8·1)*
  - *has 5 tenths (3·5)*   *– is between 4·3 and 5·3 (4·8)* *– has 4 tenths (2·4)*
  - *is between 5·8 and 6·4 (6·3)* *– is between 1·5 and 2 (1·8)*   *– is between 6·6 and 7·8 (7·2)*
  - *is between 4·1 and 4·5 (4·2)* *– has 7 tenths (2·7)*

The winners are the children still standing with 3·6 on their cards.

Who's left standing?

(continued)

Game 10: Compare numbers with two decimal places

Recognise the place value of each digit in a number with two decimal places

- Provide each child with a 'Hundredths number card'. (**Note:** Ensure you use the 12 'Hundredths number cards' provided on the CD-ROM.)

- Say: *Everyone stand up. Look at the number on your card. Sit down if the number on your card:*
  - *is between 0·56 and 2·28 (1·86)*
  - *has 5 hundredths (7·35)*
  - *is between 3·8 and 4·2 (4·07)*
  - *is between 5·48 and 5·83 (5·67)*
  - *has 1 hundredth (9·51)*
  - *is between 5·71 and 7·19 (6·94)*
  - *has 4 tenths (2·43)*
  - *is between 7·63 and 9·24 (8·19)*
  - *has 7 tenths (3·72)*
  - *is between 4·72 and 5·48 (5·23)*
  - *has 8 hundredths (0·38)*

The winners are the children still standing with 4·59 on their cards.

Game 11: Compare numbers with three decimal places

Recognise the place value of each digit in a number with three decimal places

- Provide each child with a 'Thousandths number card'. (**Note:** Ensure you use the 12 'Thousandths number cards' provided on the CD-ROM.)

- Say: *Everyone stand up. Look at the number on your card. Sit down if the number on your card:*
  - *is between 0·934 and 1·365 (1·207)*
  - *has 8 hundredths (6·782)*
  - *is between 9·5 and 10 (9·731)*
  - *has 9 thousandths (2·049)*
  - *has 7 hundredths (0·476)*
  - *is between 6·8 and 8·2 (7·965)*
  - *has 3 tenths (5·391)*
  - *is between 0·53 and 0·94 (0·835)*
  - *has 5 tenths (1·528)*
  - *is between 3·756 and 5·234 (4·613)*
  - *has 4 thousandths (3·154)*

The winners are the children still standing with 8·452 on their cards.

Forming groups

Objectives

- Read, order and compare numbers up to 1 000 000 and determine the value of each digit
- Read, order and compare numbers with up to three decimal places
- Identify the value of each digit to three decimal places

Teacher resources

- none

Pupil resources

Number cards

- '2-digit number cards', or '3-digit number cards', or '4-digit number cards', or '5-digit number cards', or '6-digit number cards', or 'tenths number cards', or 'hundredths number cards', or 'thousands number cards', or '1-12 number cards' (but only use the 1-10 number cards) (one card per child)

What to do

Game 1: Recognise the place value of each digit in any number to 1 000 000

- Using the '2-digit number cards', '3-digit number cards' and '4-digit number cards', provide each child with one card. Ensure that every child has a different number card. (**Note:** It is recommended that you use the '2-digit number cards', '3-digit number cards' and '4-digit number cards' provided on the CD-ROM.)
- Point and say: *Everyone stand up. Look at the number on your card. When I say 'Go!' I want everyone with 5 tens to move to this side of the room. Everyone with 9 ones to move to this side of the room, and everyone else to move to the back of the room. Ready? Go!*
- Once the three groups have been formed, ask the members of each group in turn to call out their numbers.

Variations

- Use different criteria to sort the numbers, for example:
  - 7 tens / 2 units / *neither* 7 tens *nor* 2 units
  - 2-digit number / 3-digit number / 4-digit number
- Use other combinations of number cards including the '5-digit number cards' and '6-digit number cards'.

Forming groups

(continued)

Game 2: Order and compare numbers to 1 000 000

- Using the '2-digit number cards', '3-digit number cards' and '4-digit number cards', provide each child with one card. Ensure that every child has a different number card. (**Note:** It is recommended that you use the '2-digit number cards', '3-digit number cards' and '4-digit number cards' provided on the CD-ROM.)

- Point and say: *Everyone stand up. Look at the number on your card. When I say 'Go!' I want everyone with a number less than 546 to move to this side of the room, and everyone with a number that is more than 546 to move to this side of the room. Ready? Go!*

- Once the two groups have been formed, ask the members of each group in turn to call out their numbers. Point and say: *Everyone hold up your number card. This group, starting with Luke, call out your numbers. Now this group, starting with Simone, tell us your numbers.*

- Then say: *As quick as you can I want each group to put yourselves in order, smallest number to largest number. Ready? Go!*

- Once the two groups have ordered their cards, ask the members of each group in turn to call out their numbers, starting with the smallest number.

Variations

- Use different criteria to order and compare the numbers, for example:

  Three groups: – less than 328   Four groups: – less than 65

                  – between 328 and 4387   – between 65 and 520

                  – more than 4387   – between 552 and 4768

                                                      – more than 4768

- Use other combinations of number cards including the '5-digit number cards' and '6-digit number cards'.

Game 3: Recognise the place value of each digit in a number with up to three decimal places

- Using the 'Tenths number cards' and 'Hundredths number cards', provide each child with one card. (**Note:** It is recommended that you use the 'Tenths number cards' and 'Hundredths number cards' provided on the CD-ROM.)

- Point and say: *Everyone stand up. Look at the number on your card. When I say 'Go!' I want everyone with 8 tenths to move to this side of the room. Everyone with 2 tenths to move to this side of the room, and everyone else to move to the back of the room. Ready? Go!*

- Once the three groups have been formed, ask the members of each group in turn to call out their numbers.

Variations

- Use just the 'Tenths number cards' or the 'Hundredths number cards'.
- Use different criteria to sort the numbers, for example:
  - 5 tenths / 8 tenths / *neither* 5 tenths *nor* 8 tenths
  - tenths number / hundredths number
- Use other combinations of number cards including the 'Thousandths number cards'.

(continued)

Forming groups

(continued)

Game 4: Order and compare numbers with up to three decimal places

- Using the 'Tenths number cards', 'Hundredths number cards' and '1–10 number cards', provide each child with one card. Use all the 'Tenths number cards' and 'Hundredths number cards' and supplement these with the '1–10 number cards' to ensure that every child has a different number card. (**Note**: It is recommended that you use the 'Tenths number cards' and 'Hundredths number cards' provided on the CD-ROM.)

- Point and say: *Everyone stand up. Look at the number on your card. When I say 'Go!' I want everyone with a number less than 6·5 to move to this side of the room, and everyone with a number that is more than 6·5 to move to this side of the room. Ready? Go!*

- Once the two groups have been formed, ask the members of each group in turn to call out their numbers. Point and say: *Everyone hold up your number card. This group, starting with Martin, call out your numbers. Now this group, starting with Louis, tell us your numbers.*

- Then say: *As quick as you can I want each group to put yourselves in order, smallest number to largest number. Ready? Go!*

- Once the two groups have ordered their cards, ask the members of each group in turn to call out their numbers, starting with the smallest number.

Variations

- Use other combinations of number cards including the 'Thousandths number cards'.
- Use different criteria to order and compare the numbers, for example:

Whole numbers: – 4 or less   Tenths: – 3·2 or less

          – between 4 and 7   – between 3·2 and 5·4

          – 7 or more   – 5·4 or more

Hundredths: – less than 4·25   Thousandths: – less than 2·225

          – between 4·25 and 6·75   – between 2·225 and 5·225

          – more than 6·75   – more than 5·225

Scientific comparisons

Objective

- Read, order and compare numbers at least to 1 000 000

Pupil resources

- *Fluency in Number Facts: Facts and Games: Years 5 & 6* book pages 44 and 45 (per pair); PDFs:

Paired games and activities → Paired games from the *Facts and Games: Years 5 & 6* book

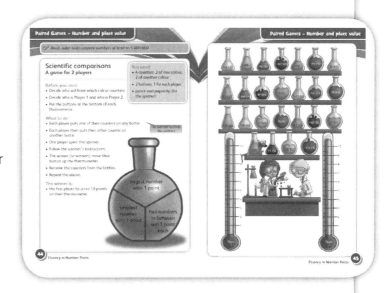

- 4 counters: 2 of one colour, 2 of another colour (per pair)
- 2 buttons: 1 for each player (per pair)
- pencil and paperclip (for the spinner) (per pair)

Notes

- Before the children play the game, ensure that they are familiar with how to use the spinner (see *Facts and Games: Years 5 & 6* book page 80).

Variations

- Children play the game in groups of three. You need six counters: two each of three different colours, and three buttons: one for each player. Use both sides of one of the thermometers.

 or

- You need 25 counters. Cover all the numbers on a bottle with a counter. Each player removes a counter from a bottle. One player spins the spinner.
  - If playing with two players: the winner keeps both counters (if 'two numbers in between…' is spun the counters are discarded)
  - If playing with three players: the winner keeps all three counters.

- Children play the game individually using three counters: two of one colour and one of a different colour. They place the three counters on three different bottles and spin the spinner. They win only if the different coloured counter matches the spinner's instructions. How few goes are needed before their button reaches 5 on the thermometer?

Stone age value

Objective

- Read numbers at least to 1 000 000 and determine the value of each digit

Pupil resources

- *Fluency in Number Facts: Facts & Games: Years 5 & 6* book pages 46 and 47 (per pair); PDFs:

Paired games and activities → Paired games from the *Facts and Games: Years 5 & 6* book

- 24 counters: 12 of one colour, 12 of another colour (per pair)
- pencil and paperclip (for the spinner) (per pair)

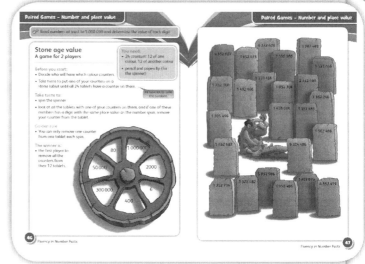

Notes

- Before the children play the game, ensure that they are familiar with how to use the spinner (see *Facts and Games: Years 5 & 6* book page 80).

Variations

- Children play the game in groups of three. You need 24 counters: eight each of three different colours.

- You need 18 counters: nine of one colour, nine of another colour. Take turns to spin the spinner and place a counter on a tablet with the smallest corresponding number, for example, spin 6, place a counter on 1 052 706. Take turns to spin the spinner again and place another counter on a corresponding tablet that is larger than the tablet previously covered. Each tablet can only have one counter on it. The loser is the first player who is unable to find a larger tablet that corresponds to their spin.

- Play the game as described in the variation above using 18 counters: six each of three different colours. The winner is the last player left in the game.

- Children play the game individually. They use 12 of the counters to cover 12 of the stone tablets. They spin the spinner and can remove a counter from one or two tablets. How few goes are needed to remove all 12 counters? They can use the other 12 counters to keep a tally of how many goes it takes them.

Cupcake value
Cupcake comparisons

Objectives

- Identify the value of each digit to three decimal places
- Read and compare numbers with up to three decimal places

Pupil resources

- *Fluency in Number Facts: Facts and Games: Years 5 & 6* book pages 48 and 49 (per pair); PDFs:

Paired games and activities → Paired games from the *Facts and Games: Years 5 & 6* book

For Cupcake value:

- 24 counters: 12 of one colour, 12 of another colour (per pair)

For Cupcake comparisons:

- about 15 counters per pair
- pencil and paperclip (for the spinner) (per pair)

Notes

- Before the children play the game, ensure that they are familiar with how to use the spinners (see *Facts and Games: Years 5 & 6* book page 80).

Variations

Cupcake value

- Children play the game in groups of three. You need 24 counters: eight each of three different colours.

- Each player places one counter on a cupcake. One player spins the spinner.
  - If there is one winner: they keep both counters.
  - If there are two winners: each player takes one of the counters.
  - If there are no winners: both counters are discarded.
- Continue for 12 goes until all 24 counters have been used.
- The winner is the player with more counters.

- Children play the game individually. They use 12 of the counters to cover 12 of the cupcakes. They spin the spinner and can remove a counter from one or two cupcakes. How few goes are needed to remove all 12 counters? They can use the other 12 counters to keep a tally of how many goes it takes them.

Cupcake comparisons

- Children play the game in groups of three.

- Children play the game individually. How few turns do they take to complete a line of four counters?

Whirlpool rounding

Objective

- Round decimals with two decimal places to the nearest whole number and to one decimal place

Pupil resources

- *Fluency in Number Facts: Facts and Games: Years 5 & 6* book pages 50 and 51 (per pair); PDFs:

 → Paired games and activities → Paired games from the *Facts and Games: Years 5 & 6* book

- 2 × 1–9 digit cards (per pair)
- about 30 counters (per pair)

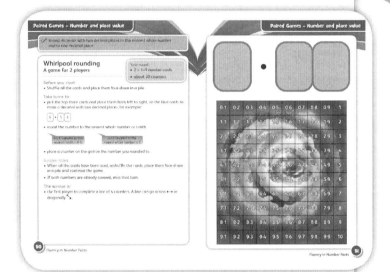

Variations

- Children play the game in groups of three.

- You need 30 counters: 15 of one colour, 15 of another colour. Once a player has turned over the three cards they are allowed to arrange the cards in any order, for example, 3 5 7 can make 3·57, 3·75, 5·37, 5·73, 7·35 or 7·53. The winner is the first player to make a line of three of their own coloured counters.

- Children play the game individually. How few turns do they take to complete a line of four counters?

Anyone for tennis?

Objective

- Multiply and divide whole numbers by 10, 100 and 1000

Pupil resources

- *Fluency in Number Facts: Facts and Games: Years 5 & 6* book pages 52 and 53 (per pair); PDFs:

Paired games and activities → Paired games from the *Facts and Games: Years 5 & 6* book

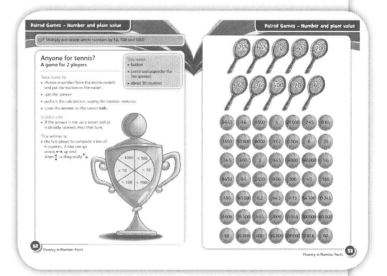

- button (per pair)
- pencil and paperclip (for the spinner) (per pair)
- about 30 counters (per pair)

Notes

- Before the children play the game, ensure that they are familiar with how to use the spinner (see *Facts and Games: Years 5 & 6* book page 80).

Variations

- Children play the game in groups of three.

or Use estimation to check answers to calculations

- One player places the button on a tennis racket. Each player places a counter on a tennis ball. One player spins the spinner. Each player performs the operation on their tennis ball number. The player with the answer nearest the racket number takes all the counters. The winner is the first player to collect 12 counters.

- Children play the game individually. If they cannot go, discard the counter. How few turns do they take to complete a line of four counters?

A night at the opera

Objective

- Multiply and divide numbers by 10 and 100 where the answers are up to three decimal places

Pupil resources

- *Fluency in Number Facts: Facts and Games: Years 5 & 6* book pages 54 and 55 (per pair); PDFs:

Paired games and activities → Paired games from the *Facts and Games: Years 5 & 6* book

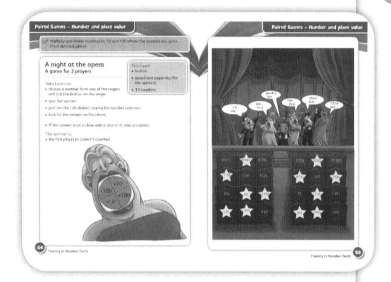

- button (per pair)
- pencil and paperclip (for the spinner) (per pair)
- 10 counters (per pair)

Notes

- Before the children play the game, ensure that they are familiar with how to use the spinner (see *Facts and Games: Years 5 & 6* book page 80).

Variations

- Children play the game in groups of three using 15 counters.

- Decide who will have the chairs on the left-hand side and who will have the chairs on the right-hand side. One player spins the spinner. Both players then find a singer's number that, when the spinner operation is performed on it, gives an answer that is on one of their starred seats, for example, ÷ 10 is spun, left-hand player: 173·8 ÷ 10 = 17·38; right-hand player: 20·6 ÷ 10 = 2·06. The first player to say their calculation takes a counter. The winner is the first player to collect 5 counters.

- Children play the game individually. If the answer is not on a chair with a star, discard one of the 10 counters. Can the child collect 5 counters before 5 counters have been discarded?

Which is larger?

Objectives

- Read, order and compare numbers up to 1 000 000
- Read, order and compare numbers with up to three decimal places

Pupil resources

Whole-class games and activities → Hands-on game boards

- 'Hands-on: 4-digit numbers' game board (per pair)
- 12 large counters (per pair)

What to do

- Cover each of the numbers on the bubbles with a counter.
- Each child then removes one counter from the bubbles.
- The child who removes the counter from the larger number keeps both counters.
- The game continues until all the counters are removed from the bubbles.
- The winner is the child with more counters.
- Play three games.

Variations

- Play 'Which is smaller?' The child who removes the counter from the smaller number keeps both counters.
- Use the 'Hands-on: 2-digit numbers' game board, 'Hands-on: 3-digit numbers' game board, 'Hands-on: 5-digit numbers' game board, 'Hands-on: 6-digit numbers' game board, 'Hands-on: 1–10 million' game board, 'Hands-on: Tenths' game board, 'Hands-on: Hundredths' game board and 'Hands-on: Thousandths' game board.

Hold it up

Objective

- Add and subtract numbers mentally with increasingly large numbers and decimals

Teacher resources

Whole-class games and activities → PowerPoint slides

- 'Hold it up'

Pupil resources

- set of 0–9 number cards or small individual whiteboard and pen (per child)

Hold it up
2-digit numbers

35	83	27	62
	71	42	94
16	58	39	74
	46	67	51

Fluency in Number Facts Years 5 & 6   www.collinseducation.com © HarperCollins Publishers Limited 2013

What to do

- Using the 'Hold it up: 2-digit numbers' slide, write an addition or subtraction operation in the box at the top of the slide, for example, 54 +.
- Point to one of the coloured numbers on the slide.
- Children work out the answer and hold up the appropriate digit card(s) / write the answer on their whiteboard.
- Repeat several times.

Variations

- Write different addition or subtraction operations in the box.
- Use the 'Hold it up: Numbers 1–10', 'Hold it up: Numbers 1–12', 'Hold it up: Numbers 1–20', 'Hold it up: 3-digit numbers', 'Hold it up: Tenths' slide and 'Hold it up: Hundredths' slide.
- Change the numbers on the 'Hold it up' slides.

Gladiators

Objective

- Add and subtract numbers mentally with increasingly large numbers and decimals

Teacher resources

Whole-class games and activities → PowerPoint slides

- 'Gladiators'

Pupil resources

- 2 × rulers or 'swords'

Gladiators
3-digit numbers

204	641	467	923	576
752	315	188	890	239
431	513	765	624	132
347	885	956	478	589

Fluency in Number Facts Years 5 & 6   www.collinseducation.com © HarperCollins*Publishers* Limited 2013

What to do

- Display the 'Gladiators 3-digit numbers' slide.
- Ask two children to stand either side of the numbers.
- Ask an addition or subtraction calculation where the answer is on the board, for example, *438 add 40 is…*
- The first child to point to the correct answer stays in. The other child sits down.
- Quickly choose another child to come and take the place of the child that just sat down.
- Continue as above.
- Which child can stay in the longest?

Variations

- The children sitting down ask the two children standing by the numbers a question where the answer is on the slide.
- To quicken the game, have two children standing either side of the numbers, one behind the other. When a child loses and has to sit down, there is an immediate replacement.
- Use the 'Gladiators: Numbers 1–20', 'Gladiators: 2-digit numbers', 'Gladiators: 2- and 3-digit multiples of 10' and 'Gladiators: 4-digit numbers' slides.
- Use the 'Gladiators: 5-digit numbers' and 'Gladiators: 6-digit numbers' slides, asking the children to add and subtract multiples of 10, 100, 1000 or 10 000.
- Use the 'Gladiators: Tenths' and 'Gladiators: Hundredths' slides, asking the children to add and subtract ones or tenths.

Hands-on

Objective

- Add and subtract numbers mentally with increasingly large numbers and decimals

Teacher resources

- none

Pupil resources

Whole-class games and activities → Hands-on game boards

- 'Hands-on' game board (per pair)

What to do

- Decide which range of numbers you want the children to use to practise and consolidate the addition and subtraction facts.
- Arrange the children into pairs and provide each pair with a copy of the appropriate 'Hands-on' game board, for example, 'Hands-on: 3-digit numbers' game board.
- Tell the children to put the game board between them and to put their index fingers on a hand at the bottom of the game board.
- Ask an appropriate addition or subtraction calculation that the children are practising, for example, *328 add 50*.
- The first child to point to the correct answer wins.
- Children keep count of how many rounds they win.
- Play for as long as is appropriate.
- The winner in each pair is the child who wins more rounds.

Variations

- Provide each pair with a pile of counters. As a child wins a game they take a counter. The winner in each pair is the child who wins more counters.
- Use the 'Hands-on: Numbers 1–20' game board, 'Hands-on: 2-digit numbers' game board, 'Hands-on: 2- and 3-digit multiples of 10' game board and 'Hands-on: 4-digit numbers' game board.
- Use the 'Hands-on: 5-digit numbers' game board and 'Hands-on: 6-digit numbers' game board, asking the children to add and subtract multiples of 10, 100, 1000 or 10 000.
- Use the 'Hands-on: Tenths' game board and 'Hands-on: Hundredths' game board, asking the children to add and subtract ones or tenths.

Bingo

Objective

- Add and subtract numbers mentally with increasingly large numbers and decimals

Teacher resources

Whole-class games and activities → PowerPoint slides

- 'Bingo'

Pupil resources

- pencil and paper or small individual whiteboard and pen (per child)

Bingo
3-digit numbers

635	391	206	713	987	429
120	872	514	658	351	253
472	957	176	820	595	784
728	319	603	231	840	144
912	405	538	767	446	649
365	283	936	164	898	587

Fluency in Number Facts Years 5 & 6   www.collinseducation.com © HarperCollinsPublishers Limited 2013

What to do

- Display the 'Bingo: 3-digit numbers' slide.
- Ask each child to write down any five numbers from the slide.
- Ask questions involving addition and subtraction where the answer is on the slide.
- Children look to find if any of their five numbers is the answer to the question.
- If a child has the answer, they cross out that number.
- The winner is the first child to cross out all five of their numbers and call out 'Bingo!'

(**Note:** Be sure to keep a record of the answers for checking purposes.)

Variations

- Ask the children to write down more or fewer than five numbers from the slide.
- Use the 'Bingo: Numbers 1–20', 'Bingo: 2-digit numbers', 'Bingo: 4-digit numbers', 'Bingo: Multiples of 10 and 100', 'Bingo: Multiples of 100 and 1000' slides.
- Use the 'Bingo: 5-digit numbers' and 'Bingo: 6-digit numbers' slides, asking the children to add and subtract multiples of 10, 100, 1000 or 10 000.
- Use the 'Bingo: Tenths' and 'Bingo: Hundredths' slides, asking the children to add and subtract ones or tenths.

Four in a row

Objective

- Add and subtract numbers mentally with increasingly large numbers and decimals

Teacher resources

Whole-class games and activities → PowerPoint slides

- 'Four in a row'
- 0–9, 1–12 or 1–20 dice

Pupil resources

- none

Four in a row
Addition and subtraction (3-digit)

792	805	216	347	635	472
124	983	461	550	872	779
680	586	305	268	924	185
237	761	142	419	847	954
458	813	624	743	391	536
329	590	963	156	658	273

Fluency in Number Facts Years 5 & 6   www.collinseducation.com © HarperCollinsPublishers Limited 2013

What to do

- Divide the class into two teams – a red team and a blue team.
- Display the 'Four in a row: Addition and subtraction (3-digit)' slide.
- Explain that the object of the game is for a team to highlight a row of four numbers either side to side, up and down or diagonally.
- To highlight a number, a team must successfully answer an addition or subtraction question.
- Invite a child from the red team to roll the dice and say the number.
- Ask an addition or subtraction question that includes the number rolled and where the answer is on the slide.
- Select a child from the red team to call out the answer.
- If correct, this number is highlighted in red on the slide. If incorrect, ask a child from the blue team to give the answer. If correct, this number is highlighted in blue.
- Next, invite a child from the blue team to roll the dice.
- Repeat the above, at a quick pace, until one team has highlighted a row of four numbers.

Variations

- Use two 0–9 dice in order to generate any 2-digit number.
- The team that rolls the dice decides what number to add to or subtract from the dice number.
- Display the 'Four in a row: Addition and subtraction (1- and 2-digit)', 'Four in a row: 2- and 3-digit multiples of 10' and 'Four in a row: Addition and subtraction (4-digit)' slides.
- Use the 'Four in a row: Tenths' and 'Four in a row: Hundredths' slides, asking the children to add and subtract ones or, if available, a tenths dice.

Tell me the facts

Objective

- Add and subtract numbers mentally with increasingly large numbers and decimals

Teacher resources

○ → ▢ → ▢

Whole-class games   PowerPoint
and activities   slides

- 'Tell me the facts'

Pupil resources

- none

Tell me the facts
Addition and subtraction to 100

13	32	73	59	16	34
86	54	26	80	69	41
91	27	42	23	95	74
49	90	67	44	50	22
78	34	15	72	98	68
65	21	58	31	87	10

Fluency in Number Facts Years 5 & 6   www.collinseducation.com © HarperCollinsPublishers Limited 2013

What to do

- Display the 'Tell me the facts: Addition and subtraction to 100' slide.

- Ask a child to highlight two numbers next to each other either side to side, up and down, or diagonally and say a known addition or subtraction number fact about these two numbers, i.e. *I know that 67 add 44 equals 111.*

- Repeat asking other children to come and highlight two other numbers, saying a known addition or subtraction number fact about the two numbers.

Variations

- Ask questions such as:
  - *Point to two numbers next to each other that have a total of 81.*
  - *Point to two numbers next to each other that have a difference of 46.*
- Use the 'Tell me the facts: Addition and subtraction to 20', 'Tell me the facts: Addition and subtraction to 1000' and 'Tell me the facts: 2- and 3-digit multiples of 10' slides.
- Use the 'Tell me the facts: Addition and subtraction (tenths)' and 'Tell me the facts: Addition and subtraction (hundredths)' slides.

Tell me your numbers

Objective

- Add and subtract numbers mentally with increasingly large numbers and decimals

Teacher resources

- none

Pupil resources

Number cards

- a 2-digit number card (per child)

What to do

- Provide each child with a 2-digit number card.
- Quickly call out two children's names.
- Both children stand and say the numbers on their cards.
- Ask these two children an appropriate addition or subtraction question using the two numbers on the cards.
- The two children sit down.
- Repeat for other pairs of children.

Variations

- Use combinations of the following number cards: '1–20 number cards', '3-digit number cards', '4-digit number cards', '5-digit number cards', '6-digit number cards, '2- and 3-digit multiples of 10 number cards' and 'Multiples of 100 and 1000 number cards'.
- Use the 'Tenths number cards' and 'Hundredths number cards'.

Who's left standing?

Objective

- Add and subtract numbers mentally with increasingly large numbers and decimals

Teacher resources

- none

Pupil resources

Number cards

- '1–20 number cards', '2-digit number cards', '3-digit number cards', '2- or 3-digit multiple of 10 number cards', 'Multiples of 100 and 1000 number cards' or 'Tenths number cards' (one card per child)

What to do

Game 1: Recall and use addition and subtraction facts to 20

- Provide each child with a 1–20 number card.
- Say: *Everyone stand up. Look at the number on your card. Sit down if the number on your card is the answer to:*
  - *17 subtract 13 (4)*
  - *the difference between 9 and 4 (5)*
  - *7 add 6 (13)*
  - *9 plus 5 (14)*
  - *the sum of 8 and 4 (12)*
  - *20 minus 9 (11)*
  - *8 add 7 (15)*
  - *12 plus 6 (18)*
  - *the difference between 9 and 8 (1)*
  - *the total of 9 and 8 (17)*
  - *9 more than 10 (19)*
  - *15 subtract 6 (9)*
  - *12 take away 9 (3)*
  - *10 add 10 (20)*
  - *15 subtract 8 (7)*
  - *3 add 5 (8)*
  - *the difference between 11 and 13 (2)*
  - *20 minus 14 (6)*
  - *the sum of 6 and 4 (10)*

The winners are the children still standing with 16 on their cards.

(*continued*)

Who's left standing?

(continued)

Game 2: Add and subtract numbers mentally, including a 2-digit number and ones

- Provide each child with a '2-digit number card'. (**Note:** Ensure you use the 12 '2-digit number cards' provided on the CD-ROM.)

- Say: *Everyone stand up. Look at the number on your card. Sit down if the number on your card is the answer to:*
  - *44 subtract 6* (38)
  - *92 add 5* (97)
  - *7 more than 66* (73)
  - *37 add 5* (42)
  - *37 minus 8* (29)
  - *30 minus 5* (25)
  - *47 add 6* (53)
  - *62 plus 8* (70)
  - *41 subtract 7* (34)
  - *4 more than 48* (52)
  - *95 subtract 9* (86)

The winners are the children still standing with 61 on their cards.

Game 3: Add and subtract numbers mentally, including a 2-digit number and tens

- Provide each child with a '2-digit number card'. (**Note:** Ensure you use the 12 '2-digit number cards' provided on the CD-ROM.)

- Say: *Everyone stand up. Look at the number on your card. Sit down if the number on your card is the answer to:*
  - *72 subtract 30* (42)
  - *36 add 50* (86)
  - *99 minus 70* (29)
  - *13 plus 40* (53)
  - *20 less than 90* (70)
  - *11 add 50* (61)
  - *50 add 47* (97)
  - *the sum of 43 and 30* (73)
  - *84 minus 50* (34)
  - *10 more than 42* (52)
  - *85 subtract 60* (25)

The winners are the children still standing with 38 on their cards.

Game 4: Add and subtract numbers mentally, including two 2-digit numbers

- Provide each child with a '2-digit number card'. (**Note:** Ensure you use the 12 '2-digit number cards' provided on the CD-ROM.)

- Say: *Everyone stand up. Look at the number on your card. Sit down if the number on your card is the answer to:*
  - *the sum of 48 and 49* (97)
  - *72 subtract 47* (25)
  - *84 minus 46* (38)
  - *25 add 36* (61)
  - *81 take away 39* (42)
  - *77 minus 43* (34)
  - *26 add 44* (70)
  - *90 subtract 37* (53)
  - *18 plus 68* (86)
  - *63 minus 34* (29)
  - *the total of 25 and 27* (52)

The winners are the children still standing with 73 on their cards.

Who's left standing?

(continued)

Game 5: Add and subtract numbers mentally, including a 3-digit number and ones

- Provide each child with a '3-digit number card'. (**Note:** Ensure you use the 12 '3-digit number cards' provided on the CD-ROM.)
- Say: *Everyone stand up. Look at the number on your card. Sit down if the number on your card is the answer to:*
  - *247 add 8 (255)*
  - *497 plus 7 (504)*
  - *324 subtract 6 (318)*
  - *466 add 5 (471)*
  - *202 subtract 9 (193)*
  - *436 minus 7 (429)*

  - *655 subtract 8 (647)*
  - *854 plus 6 (860)*
  - *4 less than 940 (936)*
  - *674 add 9 (683)*
  - *573 minus 5 (568)*

The winners are the children still standing with 735 on their cards.

Game 6: Add and subtract numbers mentally, including a 3-digit number and a multiple of ten

- Provide each child with a '3-digit number card'. (**Note:** Ensure you use the 12 '3-digit number cards' provided on the CD-ROM.)
- Say: *Everyone stand up. Look at the number on your card. Sit down if the number on your card is the answer to:*
  - *243 subtract 50 (193)*
  - *268 add 50 (318)*
  - *165 plus 90 (255)*
  - *423 add 260 (683)*
  - *591 minus 120 (471)*
  - *326 add 610 (936)*

  - *859 subtract 430 (429)*
  - *774 take away 270 (504)*
  - *215 plus 520 (735)*
  - *the sum of 450 and 410 (860)*
  - *888 subtract 320 (568)*

The winners are the children still standing with 647 on their cards.

Game 7: Add and subtract numbers mentally, including a 3-digit number and hundreds

- Provide each child with a '3-digit number card'. (**Note:** Ensure you use the 12 '3-digit number cards' provided on the CD-ROM.)
- Say: *Everyone stand up. Look at the number on your card. Sit down if the number on your card is the answer to:*
  - *829 subtract 400 (429)*
  - *500 more than 147 (647)*
  - *555 subtract 300 (255)*
  - *235 add 500 (735)*
  - *160 plus 700 (860)*
  - *336 plus 600 (936)*

  - *400 add 168 (568)*
  - *918 take away 600 (318)*
  - *483 plus 200 (683)*
  - *971 minus 500 (471)*
  - *893 subtract 700 (193)*

The winners are the children still standing with 504 on their cards.

(continued)

Who's left standing?

(continued)

Game 8: Add and subtract numbers mentally, including a 3-digit number and a 2-digit number

- Provide each child with a '3-digit number card'. (**Note:** Ensure you use the 12 '3-digit number cards' provided on the CD-ROM.)
- *Say: Everyone stand up. Look at the number on your card. Sit down if the number on your card is the answer to:*
    - *276 add 42 (318)*
    - *605 subtract 37 (568)*
    - *881 plus 55 (936)*
    - *711 subtract 64 (647)*
    - *398 add 73 (471)*
    - *562 subtract 58 (504)*
    - *674 plus 61 (735)*
    - *334 minus 79 (255)*
    - *586 plus 97 (683)*
    - *813 plus 47 (860)*
    - *241 subtract 48 (193)*

The winners are the children still standing with 429 on their cards.

Game 9: Add and subtract numbers mentally, including pairs of 2- and 3-digit multiples of 10

- Provide each child with a '2- or 3-digit multiple of 10 number card'. (**Note:** Ensure you use the 12 '2- and 3-digit multiples of 10 number cards' provided on the CD-ROM.)
- *Say: Everyone stand up. Look at the number on your card. Sit down if the number on your card is the answer to:*
    - *150 add 440 (590)*
    - *390 plus 70 (460)*
    - *730 minus 80 (650)*
    - *380 plus 360 (740)*
    - *the sum of 450 and 460 (910)*
    - *760 minus 450 (310)*
    - *510 subtract 490 (20)*
    - *650 minus 520 (130)*
    - *310 subtract 260 (50)*
    - *190 add 80 (270)*
    - *410 subtract 330 (80)*

The winners are the children still standing with 820 on their cards.

Game 10: Add and subtract numbers mentally, including multiples of 100 and 1000

- Provide each child with a 'Multiples of 100 or 1000 number card'. (**Note:** Ensure you use the 12 'Multiples of 100 and 1000 number cards' provided on the CD-ROM.)
- *Say: Everyone stand up. Look at the number on your card. Sit down if the number on your card is the answer to:*
    - *5800 subtract 4200 (1600)*
    - *1200 add 4000 (5200)*
    - *4200 subtract 3900 (300)*
    - *5700 plus 2400 (8100)*
    - *6300 subtract 4300 (2000)*
    - *4100 minus 3600 (500)*
    - *5900 add 3800 (9700)*
    - *5000 less than 9900 (4900)*
    - *1600 plus 5800 (7400)*
    - *the difference between 2300 and 3100 (800)*
    - *2400 plus 3600 (6000)*

The winners are the children still standing with 3000 on their cards.

Who's left standing?

(continued)

Game 11: Add decimals mentally: U·t + U·t

- Provide each child with a 'Tenths number card'. (**Note:** Ensure you use the 12 'Tenths number cards' provided on the CD-ROM.)
- Say: *Everyone stand up. Look at the number on your card. Sit down if the number on your card is the answer to:*
  - *0·8 add 1·9 (2·7)*
  - *3·5 plus 2·8 (6·3)*
  - *the sum of 4·9 and 3·2 (8·1)*
  - *0·6 add 0·6 (1·2)*
  - *1·7 plus 1·9 (3·6)*
  - *0·5 plus 1·3 (1·8)*
  - *1·6 add 2·6 (4·2)*
  - *1·7 plus 3·9 (5·6)*
  - *1·6 add 0·8 (2·4)*
  - *2·5 plus 2·3 (4·8)*
  - *4·7 add 2·5 (7·2)*

The winners are the children still standing with 3·5 on their cards.

Game 12: Subtract decimals mentally: U·t – U·t

- Provide each child with a 'Tenths number card'. (**Note:** Ensure you use the 12 'Tenths number cards' provided on the CD-ROM.)
- Say: *Everyone stand up. Look at the number on your card. Sit down if the number on your card is the answer to:*
  - *9·2 subtract 5·7 (3·5)*
  - *7·1 minus 1·5 (5·6)*
  - *8·3 subtract 1·1 (7·2)*
  - *2·4 minus 0·6 (1·8)*
  - *6·5 subtract 2·9 (3·6)*
  - *0·8 less than 8·9 (8·1)*
  - *the difference between 3·7 and 2·5 (1·2)*
  - *5·8 minus 3·4 (2·4)*
  - *6·5 subtract 1·7 (4·8)*
  - *3·4 minus 0·7 (2·7)*
  - *9·1 subtract 2·8 (6·3)*

The winners are the children still standing with 4·2 on their cards.

Game 13: Add and subtract decimals mentally: U·t ± U·t

- Provide each child with a 'Tenths number card'. (**Note:** Ensure you use the 12 'Tenths number cards' provided on the CD-ROM.)
- Say: *Everyone stand up. Look at the number on your card. Sit down if the number on your card is the answer to:*
  - *5·6 add 2·5 (8·1)*
  - *6·1 subtract 4·9 (1·2)*
  - *3·8 plus 3·4 (7·2)*
  - *5·2 minus 3·4 (1·8)*
  - *7·5 subtract 5·1 (2·4)*
  - *1·3 add 3·5 (4·8)*
  - *8·3 minus 5·6 (2·7)*
  - *4·4 minus 0·9 (3·5)*
  - *1·7 plus 2·5 (4·2)*
  - *5·4 subtract 1·8 (3·6)*
  - *5·5 plus 0·8 (6·3)*

The winners are the children still standing with 5·6 on their cards.

Stand up

Objective

- Add and subtract numbers mentally with increasingly large numbers and decimals

Teacher resources

- none

Pupil resources

Number cards

- '1–12 number cards', '2-digit number cards', '3-digit number cards', '2- or 3-digit multiple of 10 number cards', 'Multiple of 100 or 1000 number cards' or 'Tenths number cards' (one card per child)

What to do

Game 1: Recall and use addition and subtraction facts to 20

- Provide each child with a '1–12 number card'.
- Say: *Look at the number on your card. Stand up if your card shows the answer to 15 subtract 11.*
- Ask: *Who can tell me what number is on Cryder's and Vernon's cards?* (4)
- Ask the children standing to show their cards.
- The children standing then sit down.
- Repeat for the following:
  - *Stand up if your card shows the answer to 15 subtract 4.* (11)
  - *Stand up if your card shows the answer to 14 take away 8.* (6)
  - *Add 15 to the number on your card. If the sum is 18, stand up.* (3)
  - *Add 5 to the number on your card. If the answer is 17, stand up.* (12)
  - *Stand up if your card shows the answer to 20 minus 11.* (9)
  - *Add 7 to the number on your card. If the answer is 12, stand up.* (5)
  - *Add 12 to the number on your card. If the total is 14, stand up.* (2)
  - *Stand up if your card shows the answer to 16 subtract 8.* (8)
  - *Add 11 to the number on your card. If the answer is 18, stand up.* (7)
  - *Stand up if your card shows the difference between 14 and 15.* (1)
  - *Add 8 to the number on your card. If the sum is 18, stand up.* (10)

Stand up

(continued)

Game 2: Add and subtract numbers mentally, including a 2-digit number and ones

- Provide each child with a '2-digit number card'. (**Note:** Ensure you use the 12 '2-digit number cards' provided on the CD-ROM.)
- Say: *Look at the number on your card. Add 8 to the number on your card. If the total is 61, stand up.*
- Ask: *Who can tell me what number is on Faith's and Rochelle's cards?* (53)
- Ask the children standing to show their cards.
- The children standing then sit down.
- Repeat for the following:
  - *Add 9 to the number on your card. If the total is 51, stand up.* (42)
  - *Stand up if your card shows the answer to 37 minus 8.* (29)
  - *Add 7 to the number on your card. If the total is 68, stand up.* (61)
  - *Stand up if the number on your card is 5 less than 43.* (38)
  - *Add 6 to the number on your card. If the answer is 31, stand up.* (25)
  - *Add 8 to the number on your card. If the total is 78, stand up.* (70)
  - *Stand up if your card shows the answer to 43 take away 9.* (34)
  - *Add 5 to the number on your card. If the sum is 102, stand up.* (97)
  - *Stand up if your card shows the answer to 81 subtract 8.* (73)
  - *Add 9 to the number on your card. If the total is 61, stand up.* (52)
  - *Stand up if your card shows the answer to 92 subtract 6.* (86)

Game 3: Add and subtract numbers mentally, including a 2-digit number and tens

- Provide each child with a '2-digit number card'. (**Note:** Ensure you use the 12 '2-digit number cards' provided on the CD-ROM.)
- Say: *Look at the number on your card. Stand up if your card shows the answer to 72 take away 20.*
- Ask: *Who can tell me what number is on Chloe's and Taylah's cards?* (52)
- Ask the children standing to show their cards.
- The children standing then sit down.
- Repeat for the following:
  - *Add 30 to the number on your card. If the answer is 91, stand up.* (61)
  - *Add 10 to the number on your card. If the total is 96, stand up.* (86)
  - *Stand up if your card shows the answer to 75 minus 50.* (25)
  - *Add 20 to the number on your card. If the total is 90, stand up.* (70)
  - *Stand up if your card shows the answer to 88 subtract 50.* (38)
  - *Add 40 to the number on your card. If the total is 137, stand up.* (97)
  - *Stand up if your card shows the answer to 72 minus 30.* (42)
  - *Add 80 to the number on your card. If the total is 153, stand up.* (73)
  - *Add 50 to the number on your card. If the answer is 103, stand up.* (53)
  - *Stand up if your card shows the answer to 69 minus 40.* (29)
  - *Stand up if your card shows the answer to 94 subtract 60.* (34)

(continued)

Stand up

(continued)

Game 4: Add and subtract numbers mentally, including two 2-digit numbers

- Provide each child with a '2-digit number card'. (**Note:** Ensure you use the 12 '2-digit number cards' provided on the CD-ROM.)
- Say: *Look at the number on your card. Stand up if your card shows the answer to 82 subtract 29.*
- Ask: *Who can tell me what number is on Pascal's and Olivia's cards?* (53)
- Ask the children standing to show their cards.
- The children standing then sit down.
- Repeat for the following:
  - *Add 39 to the number on your card. If the total is 100, stand up.* (61)
  - *Stand up if your card shows the answer to 83 take away 58.* (25)
  - *Add 46 to the number on your card. If the sum is 98, stand up.* (52)
  - *Stand up if your card shows the answer to 61 subtract 27.* (34)
  - *Add 18 to the number on your card. If the total is 104, stand up.* (86)
  - *Stand up if your card shows the answer to 93 minus 55.* (38)
  - *Add 25 to the number on your card. If the answer is 98, stand up.* (73)
  - *Add 52 to the number on your card. If the answer is 149, stand up.* (97)
  - *Stand up if your card shows the answer to 74 take away 32.* (42)
  - *Add 18 to the number on your card. If the total is 88, stand up.* (70)
  - *Stand up if your card shows the answer to 52 subtract 23.* (29)

Game 5: Add and subtract numbers mentally, including a 3-digit number and ones

- Provide each child with a '3-digit number card'. (**Note:** Ensure you use the 12 '3-digit number cards' provided on the CD-ROM.)
- Say: *Look at the number on your card. Add 7 to the number on your card. If the total is 654, stand up.*
- Ask: *Who can tell me what number is on Luke's and Sandeep's cards?* (647)
- Ask the children standing to show their cards.
- The children standing then sit down.
- Repeat for the following:
  - *Stand up if your card shows the answer to 201 minus 8.* (193)
  - *Add 9 to the number on your card. If the answer is 692, stand up.* (683)
  - *Add 5 to the number on your card. If the answer is 865, stand up.* (860)
  - *Stand up if your card shows the answer to 943 take away 7.* (936)
  - *Add 6 to the number on your card. If the total is 324, stand up.* (318)
  - *Stand up if your card shows the answer to 513 subtract 9.* (504)
  - *Add 8 to the number on your card. If the total is 263, stand up.* (255)
  - *Stand up if your card shows the answer to 477 take away 6.* (471)
  - *Add 4 to the number on your card. If the sum is 572, stand up.* (568)
  - *Stand up if your card shows the answer to 740 subtract 5.* (735)
  - *Add 7 to the number on your card. If the total is 436, stand up.* (429)

Stand up

(continued)

Game 6: Add and subtract numbers mentally, including a 3-digit number and a multiple of ten

- Provide each child with a '3-digit number card'. (**Note:** Ensure you use the 12 '3-digit number cards' provided on the CD-ROM.)
- Say: *Look at the number on your card. Stand up if your card has the answer to 975 subtract 240.*
- Ask: *Who can tell me what number is on Mel's and Robbie's cards?* (735)
- Ask the children standing to show their cards.
- The children standing then sit down.
- Repeat for the following:
  - *Add 250 to the number on your card. If the answer is 818, stand up.* (568)
  - *Stand up if your card shows the answer to 859 subtract 430.* (429)
  - *Add 430 to the number on your card. If the total is 934, stand up.* (504)
  - *Stand up if your card shows the answer to 335 minus 80.* (255)
  - *Add 360 to the number on your card. If the total is 678, stand up.* (318)
  - *Stand up if your card shows the answer to 110 less than 970.* (860)
  - *Add 40 to the number on your card. If the sum is 976, stand up.* (936)
  - *Stand up if your card shows the answer to 653 take away 460.* (193)
  - *Add 480 to the number on your card. If the total is 951, stand up.* (471)
  - *Stand up if your card shows the answer to 797 subtract 150.* (647)
  - *Add 170 to the number on your card. If the answer is 853, stand up.* (683)

Game 7: Add and subtract numbers mentally, including a 3-digit number and hundreds

- Provide each child with a '3-digit number card'. (**Note:** Ensure you use the 12 '3-digit number cards' provided on the CD-ROM.)
- Say: *Look at the number on your card. Add 300 to the number on your card. If the total is 868, stand up.*
- Ask: *Who can tell me what number is on Yolanda's and Ursula's cards?* (568)
- Ask the children standing to show their cards.
- The children standing then sit down.
- Repeat for the following:
  - *Stand up if your card shows the answer to 718 subtract 400.* (318)
  - *Add 500 to the number on your card. If the total is 971, stand up.* (471)
  - *Stand up if your card shows the answer to 947 take away 300.* (647)
  - *Add 200 to the number on your card. If the sum is 935, stand up.* (735)
  - *Stand up if your card shows the answer to 793 minus 600.* (193)
  - *Add 100 to the number on your card. If the answer is 960, stand up.* (860)
  - *Stand up if your card shows the answer to 755 subtract 500.* (255)
  - *Add 300 to the number on your card. If the answer is 983, stand up.* (683)
  - *Stand up if your card shows the answer to 804 take away 300.* (504)
  - *Add 400 to the number on your card. If the total is 1336, stand up.* (936)
  - *Stand up if your card shows the answer to 829 subtract 400.* (429)

(continued)

Stand up

(continued)

Game 8: Add and subtract numbers mentally, including a 3-digit number and a 2-digit number

- Provide each child with a '3-digit number card'. (**Note:** Ensure you use the 12 '3-digit number cards' provided on the CD-ROM.)
- Say: *Look at the number on your card. Stand up if your card shows the answer to 464 minus 35.*
- Ask: *Who can tell me what number is on Sally's and Jill's cards?* (429)
- Ask the children standing to show their cards.
- The children standing then sit down.
- Repeat for the following:
  - *Add 37 to the number on your card. If the total is 541, stand up.* (504)
  - *Stand up if your card shows the answer to 783 subtract 48.* (735)
  - *Add 76 to the number on your card. If the total is 936, stand up.* (860)
  - *Stand up if your card shows the answer to 260 take away 67.* (193)
  - *Add 55 to the number on your card. If the sum is 702, stand up.* (647)
  - *Stand up if your card shows the answer to 972 subtract 36.* (936)
  - *Add 84 to the number on your card. If the total is 652, stand up.* (568)
  - *Stand up if your card shows the answer to 373 minus 55.* (318)
  - *Add 48 to the number on your card. If the answer is 731, stand up.* (683)
  - *Add 63 to the number on your card. If the answer is 534, stand up.* (471)
  - *Stand up if your card shows the answer to 304 take away 49.* (255)

Game 9: Add and subtract numbers mentally, including pairs of 2- and 3-digit multiples of 10

- Provide each child with a '2- or 3-digit multiple of 10 number card'. (**Note:** Ensure you use the 12 '2- and 3-digit multiples of 10 number cards' provided on the CD-ROM.)
- Say: *Look at the number on your card. Add 270 to the number on your card. If the sum is 730, stand up.*
- Ask: *Who can tell me what number is on Vijay's and Paul's cards?* (460)
- Ask the children standing to show their cards.
- The children standing then sit down.
- Repeat for the following:
  - *Stand up if your card shows the answer to 430 minus 380.* (50)
  - *Add 260 to the number on your card. If the answer is 850, stand up.* (590)
  - *Stand up if your card shows the answer to 640 subtract 560.* (80)
  - *Stand up if your card shows the answer to 310 take away 40.* (270)
  - *Add 180 to the number on your card. If the total is 830, stand up.* (650)
  - *Stand up if your card shows the answer to 820 subtract 690.* (130)
  - *Add 50 to the submber on your card. If the total is 790, stand up.* (740)
  - *Stand up if your card shows the answer to 770 take away 460.* (310)
  - *Add 60 to the number on your card. If the sum is 970, stand up.* (910)
  - *Stand up if your card shows the answer to 530 subtract 510.* (20)
  - *Add 150 to the number on your card. If the total is 970, stand up.* (820)

Stand up

(continued)

Game 10: Add and subtract numbers mentally, including multiples of 100 and 1000

- Provide each child with a 'Multiple of 100 or 1000 number card'. (**Note:** Ensure you use the 12 'Multiples of 100 and 1000 number cards' provided on the CD-ROM.)
- Say: *Look at the number on your card. Stand up if your card shows the answer to 5800 minus 2800.*
- Ask: *Who can tell me what number is on Brian's and Mustafa's cards?* (3000)
- Ask the children standing to show their cards.
- The children standing then sit down.
- Repeat for the following:
  - *Stand up if your card shows the answer to 4200 minus 3900.* (300)
  - *Add 4800 to the number on your card. If the answer is 6800, stand up.* (2000)
  - *Add 1500 to the number on your card. If the answer is 8900, stand up.* (7400)
  - *Stand up if your card shows the answer to 1600 take away 1100.* (500)
  - *Add 1600 to the number on your card. If the total is 9700, stand up.* (8100)
  - *Stand up if your card shows the answer to 5800 subtract 5000.* (800)
  - *Add 7000 to the number on your card. If the total is 8600, stand up.* (1600)
  - *Stand up if your card shows the answer to 6600 take away 600.* (6000)
  - *Add 200 to the number on your card. If the sum is 9900, stand up.* (9700)
  - *Stand up if your card shows the answer to 7600 subtract 2400.* (5200)
  - *Add 3700 to the number on your card. If the total is 8600, stand up.* (4900)

Game 11: Add decimals mentally: U·t + U·t

- Provide each child with a tenths number card. (**Note:** Ensure you use the 12 'Tenths number cards' provided on the CD-ROM.)
- Say: *Look at the number on your card. Add 1·6 to the number on your card. If the sum is 5·1, stand up.*
- Ask: *Who can tell me what number is on Sanjay's and Lee's cards?* (3·5)
- Ask the children standing to show their cards.
- The children standing then sit down.
- Repeat for the following:
  - *Add 0·8 to the number on your card. If the answer is 3·2, stand up.* (2·4)
  - *Add 1·9 to the number on your card. If the sum is 8·2, stand up.* (6·3)
  - *Add 3·5 to the number on your card. If the total is 7·7, stand up.* (4·2)
  - *Add 2·7 to the number on your card. If the answer is 3·9, stand up.* (1·2)
  - *Add 1·8 to the number on your card. If the sum is 7·4, stand up.* (5·6)
  - *Add 0·4 to the number on your card. If the total is 8·5, stand up.* (8·1)
  - *Add 2·3 to the number on your card. If the answer is 7·1, stand up.* (4·8)
  - *Add 4·6 to the number on your card. If the sum is 6·4, stand up.* (1·8)
  - *Add 1·5 to the number on your card. If the total is 5·1, stand up.* (3·6)
  - *Add 2·8 to the number on your card. If the total is 10, stand up.* (7·2)
  - *Add 3·9 to the number on your card. If the answer is 6·6, stand up.* (2·7)

(continued)

Stand up

(continued)

Game 12: Subtract decimals mentally: U·t – U·t

- Provide each child with a tenths number card. (**Note:** Ensure you use the 12 'Tenths number cards' provided on the CD-ROM.)
- Say: *Look at the number on your card. Stand up if your card shows the answer to 4·5 subtract 1·8.*
- Ask: *Who can tell me what number is on Robert's and Richard's cards?* (2·7)
- Ask the children standing to show their cards.
- The children standing then sit down.
- Repeat for the following:
  - *Stand up if your card shows the answer to 6·5 take away 2·3.* (4·2)
  - *Stand up if your card shows the answer to 7·7 minus 1·4.* (6·3)
  - *Stand up if your card shows the difference between 4·2 and 0·7.* (3·5)
  - *Stand up if your card shows the answer to 8·4 subtract 3·6.* (4·8)
  - *Stand up if your card shows the difference between 8 and 0·8.* (7·2)
  - *Stand up if your card shows the answer to 3·1 minus 1·9.* (1·2)
  - *Stand up if your card shows the answer to 9·2 take away 5·6.* (3·6)
  - *Stand up if your card shows the answer to 6·3 subtract 0·7.* (5·6)
  - *Stand up if your card shows the answer to 5·2 minus 2·8.* (2·4)
  - *Stand up if your card shows the difference between 9·6 and 1·5.* (8·1)
  - *Stand up if your card shows the answer to 2·4 subtract 0·6.* (1·8)

Game 13: Add and subtract decimals mentally: U·t ± U·t

- Provide each child with a tenths number card. (**Note:** Ensure you use the 12 'Tenths number cards' provided on the CD-ROM.)
- Say: *Look at the number on your card. Add 2·7 to the number on your card. If the answer is 8·3, stand up.*
- Ask: *Who can tell me what number is on April's and May's cards?* (5·6)
- Ask the children standing to show their cards.
- The children standing then sit down.
- Repeat for the following:
  - *Stand up if your card shows the answer to 2·7 take away 1·5.* (1·2)
  - *Add 3·5 to the number on your card. If the answer is 8·3, stand up.* (4·8)
  - *Stand up if your card shows the answer to 5·1 minus 1·6.* (3·5)
  - *Add 1·9 to the number on your card. If the sum is 6·1, stand up.* (4·2)
  - *Stand up if your card shows the difference between 3·2 and 1·4.* (1·8)
  - *Stand up if your card shows the answer to 7·4 subtract 3·8.* (3·6)
  - *Add 0·9 to the number on your card. If the total is 8·1, stand up.* (7·2)
  - *Stand up if your card shows the difference between 3·1 and 0·7.* (2·4)
  - *Add 2·8 to the number on your card. If the sum is 9·1, stand up.* (6·3)
  - *Stand up if your card shows the answer to 5·5 subtract 2·8.* (2·7)
  - *Add 1·1 to the number on your card. If the total is 9·2, stand up.* (8·1)

Whole-class, paired or individual activities

Using the Maths Facts in the *Facts and Games* book

Objectives

* Recall and use addition and subtraction facts to 20 fluently, and derive and use related facts up to 100
* Add and subtract numbers mentally with increasingly large numbers and decimals

Teacher resources

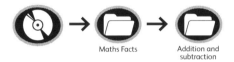

Pupil resources

* *Fluency in Number Facts: Facts and Games: Years 5 & 6* book pages 4–18 (per child or pair)

Introduction

The Maths Facts on pages 4–18 of the *Fluency in Number Facts: Facts and Games: Years 5 & 6* book cover the key addition and subtraction number facts that children should be able to recall instantly by the end of Upper Key Stage 2.

These pages aim to develop children's fluency by:

* securing a thorough conceptual understanding of the addition and subtraction number facts
* identifying patterns and the relationship between addition and subtraction
* developing strategic approaches to recalling and deriving the answers to addition and subtraction number facts.

To assist in achieving these aims, the addition and subtraction number facts contained in the *Facts and Games: Years 5 & 6* book are presented in the following ways:

* Addition and subtraction numbers facts to 20 (pages 4 and 5)
* Addition and subtraction trios to 20 (pages 6–12)
* Addition number facts to 10 and 20 table (page 13)
* Addition of 1-digit and 2-digit numbers to 20 tables (page 14)
* Multiples of 10 addition and subtraction tables (pages 15 and 16)
* Decimals addition and subtraction tables (pages 17 and 18)

The following pages include a brief description of each of these presentations, along with suggestions of how to focus on these Maths Facts either with the whole class, or with children working in pairs or individually.

(*continued*)

Whole-class, paired or individual activities

Using the Maths Facts in the *Facts and Games* book

(continued)

Addition and subtraction numbers facts to 20 (pages 4 and 5)

The facts are organised into 'number fact families', for example, Number facts for 17, which are presented in two columns – an addition column and a subtraction column. This presentation shows the number pattern in each addition and subtraction 'family' as well as the relationship between the addition and the subtraction number facts.

At this stage, children should be able to recall all the addition and subtraction facts to 20 fluently, and use these facts to derive related facts involving multiples of 10 and 100, as well as those involving decimals.

How to use the Maths Facts

 Whole class

- Display the appropriate PDF file (CD-ROM / Maths Facts / Addition and subtraction) and provide each child or pair with a copy of the *Facts and Games: Years 5 & 6* book and direct their attention to one of the 'number fact families' on pages 4 and 5.

- Begin by asking the children to identify different patterns and relationships in the lists of calculations and discuss these with the class.

- Discuss with the children how knowing the addition and subtraction number facts to 20 can help them derive answers to related number facts involving:
  - multiples of 10 and 100, for example: 4 + 13 = 17, therefore 40 + 130 = 170 and 400 + 1300 = 1700; 17 – 13 = 4, therefore 170 – 130 = 40 and 1700 – 1300 = 400
  - decimals, for example: 4 + 13 = 17, therefore 0·4 + 1·3 = 1·7 and 0·04 + 0·13 = 0·17; 17 – 13 = 4, therefore 1·7 – 1·3 = 0·4 and 0·17 – 0·13 = 0·04.

- Repeat for other addition and subtraction number facts and the related facts involving multiples of 10 and 100, as well as those involving decimals.

- Conclude by hiding the PDF file, asking the children to close their copy of the *Facts and Games: Years 5 & 6* book and ask the class questions similar to the following:
  - *What is 9 add 8?*
  - *How many more do you need to add to 4 to make 17?*
  - *12 and what other number total 17?*
  - *If 9 add 8 is 17, then what is 90 add 80? What about 900 add 800? What about 0·9 add 0·8? What about 0·09 add 0·08?*
  - *What is 17 subtract 12?*
  - *If 17 subtract 12 is 5, then what is 170 subtract 120? What about 1700 subtract 1200? What about 1·7 subtract 1·2? What about 0·17 subtract 0·12?*
  - *What is 170 subtract 60? How do you know?*
  - *What is 0·6 add 0·8? How do you know?*

Using the Maths Facts in the *Facts and Games* book

(continued)

 Pairs

- Provide each pair with a copy of the *Facts and Games: Years 5 & 6* book and direct their attention to the 'number fact families' on pages 4 and 5.
- Children spend just two or three minutes individually looking at the addition and subtraction facts with the aim of developing greater fluency of the facts.
- Children then take turns to take charge of the book and ask each other questions similar to those on page 66, including those involving multiples of 10 and 100, as well as those involving decimals.

 Individual

- Provide the child with a copy of the *Facts and Games: Years 5 & 6* book and direct their attention to the 'number fact families' on pages 4 and 5.
- It is recommended that the child spends just five or ten minutes each time, focussing their attention on developing greater fluency of the facts.
- To provide some personal challenge, suggest the child:
  - covers the number facts with their hand and recites the facts to themselves
  - recalls the related facts involving multiples of 10 and 100, as well as those involving decimals.

(*continued*)

Whole-class, paired or individual activities

Using the Maths Facts in the *Facts and Games* book

(continued)

Addition and subtraction trios to 20 (pages 6–12)

'Trios' show the relationship between the three numbers that make up an addition fact and the related subtraction fact. They also show that addition of two numbers can be done in any order (commutative) and how this law does *not* apply to subtraction.

At this stage, children should be able to recall all the addition and subtraction facts to 20 fluently, and use these facts to derive related facts involving multiples of 10 and 100, as well as those involving decimals.

How to use the Maths Facts

 Whole class

- Display the appropriate PDF file (CD-ROM / Maths Facts / Addition and subtraction) and provide each child or pair with a copy of the *Facts and Games: Years 5 & 6* book and direct their attention to the relevant 'trios' on pages 6–12.

- Begin by asking the children to identify different patterns and relationships between the four calculations in the first trio.

- Ensure the children realise that each trio consists of only three numbers, i.e. 12, 5 and 17, and that these three numbers produce four calculations: two addition calculations (12 + 5 = 17 and 5 + 12 = 17), and two subtraction calculations (17 − 5 = 12 and 17 − 12 = 5).

- Referring to the two addition calculations, remind the children how addition of two numbers can be done in any order (commutative law).

- Then, referring to the two subtraction calculations, remind the children how the commutative law does *not* apply to subtraction.

- Move on to reminding children of the inverse relationship between addition and subtraction.

- Repeat the above for remaining trios in the set.

- Discuss with the children how knowing the addition and subtraction number facts to 20 can help them derive answers to related number facts involving:
  - multiples of 10 and 100, for example: 12 + 5 = 17, therefore 120 + 50 = 170 and 1200 + 500 = 1700; 17 − 5 = 12, therefore 170 − 50 = 120 and 1700 − 500 = 1200
  - decimals, for example: 12 + 5 = 17, therefore 1·2 + 0·5 = 1·7 and 0·12 + 0·05 = 0·17; 17 − 5 = 12, therefore 1·7 − 0·5 = 1·2 and 0·17 − 0·05 = 0·12.

- Repeat for other addition and subtraction number facts and the related facts involving multiples of 10 and 100, as well as those involving decimals.

Whole-class, paired or individual activities

Using the Maths Facts in the *Facts and Games* book

(continued)

- Conclude by hiding the PDF file, asking the children to close their copy of the *Facts and Games: Years 5 & 6* book and ask the class questions similar to the following:
  - *Tell me an addition calculation you can make using only the numbers 11, 6 and 17.*
  - *Can you tell me another addition calculation that only uses the same three numbers?*
  - *Tell me a subtraction calculation that only uses the numbers 11, 6 and 17.*
  - *Is there another subtraction calculation that only uses these numbers?*
  - *If 17 subtract 8 is 9, what is 17 subtract 9? What is 170 subtract 80? What about 1700 subtract 800? What is the answer to 1·7 subtract 0·8? What about 0·17 subtract 0·08?*
  - *If you know that 11 add 6 is 17 what addition calculations involving multiples of 10 do you also know? What other addition calculations do you know? What about addition calculations involving multiples of 100? What about those involving decimals?*

 Pairs

- Provide each pair with a copy of the *Facts and Games: Years 5 & 6* book and direct their attention to the addition and subtraction 'trios' on pages 6–12.

- Children take turns to choose one of the trios and place their hand / fingers over the list of four calculations.

- Referring to the three numbers on the triangle, the other child has to say the two addition and two subtraction number facts.

- Once they have done this, the child covering the facts removes their hand / fingers to reveal the four calculations.

- Vary the activity by asking children to ask each other questions involving multiples of 10 and 100, as well as those involving decimals.

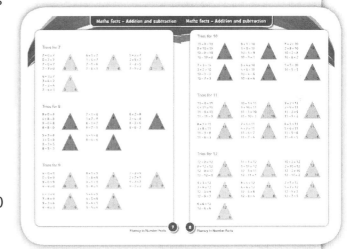

 Individual

- Provide each child with a copy of the *Facts and Games: Years 5 & 6* book and direct their attention to the addition and subtraction trios on pages 6–12.

- It is recommended that the child spends just five or ten minutes each time, focussing their attention on one set of addition and subtraction trios with the aim of developing greater fluency of the facts.

- To provide some personal challenge, as for the paired activity above, suggest the child:
  - places their hand / fingers over the list of four calculations and recites the facts to themselves
  - recalls the related facts involving multiples of 10 and 100, as well as those involving decimals.

(continued)

Whole-class, paired or individual activities

Using the Maths Facts in the *Facts and Games* book

(continued)

Addition number facts to 10 and 20 table (page 13)

Addition of 1-digit and 2-digit numbers to 20 table (page 14)

Multiples of 10 addition and subtraction tables (pages 15 and 16)

Decimals addition and subtraction tables (pages 17 and 18)

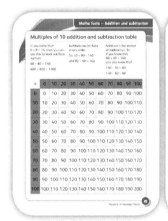
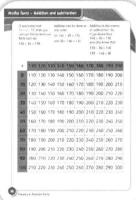

The table on page 13 shows all of the addition number facts to 20 involving the numbers 0 to 10. The answers in blue are all the number facts to 10, and the answers in green are all the number facts from 11 to 20. The table therefore, shows the progressive nature of the number facts from 0 to 20.

The table on page 14 shows all of the addition number facts to 20 involving the 1 to 9 digits and the 'teen' numbers.

The two tables on pages 15 and 16 show all of the addition number facts for the multiples of 10 from 10 to 200. These tables mirror the 'Addition number facts to 10 and 20 table' and the 'Addition of 1-digit and 2-digit numbers to 20' table on pages 13 and 14.

The two tables on pages 17 and 18 show how the 'Addition number facts 10 and 20 table' relates in tenths and hundredths.

At this stage, children should be able to recall all the addition and subtraction facts to 20 fluently, and use these facts to derive related facts involving multiples of 10 and 100, as well as those involving decimals.

All the tables also show that addition of two numbers can be done in any order (commutative) and that addition is the opposite (inverse) of subtraction.

Whole-class, paired or individual activities

Using the Maths Facts in the *Facts and Games* book

(continued)

How to use the Maths Facts

 Whole class

- Display the appropriate PDF file (CD-ROM / Maths Facts / Addition and subtraction) and provide each child or pair with a copy of the *Facts and Games: Years 5 & 6* book and direct their attention to the two tables on pages 13 and 14.
- Begin by discussing the 'Addition number facts to 10 and 20 table' on page 13 with the children. Ask them to identify different patterns and relationships in the table and discuss these with the class. Draw their attention to the patterns of numbers in each row, column and diagonal. In particular, highlight the row of numbers at the top of the table and the column of numbers down the left-hand side of the table.
- If necessary, remind the children how to use the table. Put one finger on 8 in the column of numbers down the left-hand side of the table and another finger on 9 in the row of numbers at the top of the table, and then move both fingers across and down the table until they meet at the answer, i.e. 17.
- Discuss with the children how 8 + 9 is the same as 9 + 8 (commutative).
- Repeat several times.
- Once the children are secure with reading the table for addition, remind them how the table can also be used for subtraction. Put one finger on 8 in the column of numbers down the left-hand side of the table, and then move another finger across the row until you land on 17. Once your finger is on 17, move up the column until you land on 9 in the row of numbers at the top of the table.
- Discuss with the children that if they know that 8 + 9 = 17 then they also know that 17 − 8 = 9 and 17 − 9 = 8.
- Repeat several times.
- Repeat the above for the 'Addition of 1-digit and 2-digit numbers to 20' table on page 14
- Ensure children realise that having instant recall of the addition and subtraction number facts to 20 can help them derive answers to related facts. The tables on pages 15–18 assist in developing this understanding and recall. It is recommended that teachers introduce these tables to the children during different sessions.

Multiples of 10 addition and subtraction tables

- Draw children's attention to the two 'Multiples of 10 addition and subtraction tables' on pages 15 and 16 and display the relevant PDF. Discuss with the children the similarities between the tables on pages 13 and 14, and the tables on pages 15 and 16 (although the table on page 16 extends to answers from 200 to 300).
- Highlight the following to the children:
  - The tables on pages 15 and 16 show all of the addition number facts for the multiples of 10 from 10 to 200.
  - If you know that 14 + 3 = 17 (as shown on the table on page 14), then you also know that 140 + 30 = 170 (as shown on the table on page 16).
  - Addition can be done in any order, so 140 + 30 = 170 and 30 + 140 = 170.
  - Addition is the inverse of subtraction, so if you know that 140 + 30 = 170 you also know that 170 − 30 = 140 and 170 − 140 = 30.

(continued)

Using the Maths Facts in the *Facts and Games* book

(continued)

Decimals addition and subtraction tables

- Draw children's attention to the two 'Decimals addition and subtraction tables' on pages 17 and 18 and display the relevant PDF. Discuss with the children the similarities between these two tables and the table on page 13.
- Highlight the following to the children:
  - The table on page 17 shows the related number facts involving tenths.
  - The table on page 18 shows the related number facts involving hundredths.
  - If you know that $4 + 8 = 12$ (as shown on the table on page 13), then you also know that $0·4 + 0·8 = 1·2$ (as shown on the table on page 17) and that $0·04 + 0·08 = 0·12$ (as shown on the table on page 18).
  - Addition can be done in any order, so $0·4 + 0·8 = 1·2$ and $0·8 + 0·4 = 1·2$.
  - Addition is the inverse of subtraction, so if you know that $0·4 + 0·8 = 1·2$ you also know that: $1·2 − 0·4 = 0·8$ and $1·2 − 0·8 = 0·4$.

- Referring to the relevant PDF file on display, conclude by asking the class questions similar to the following:
  - *If we know that 5 add 9 is 14, what is the answer to 50 add 90? How does the table help us check? What about 0·5 add 0·9?*
  - *If we know that 7 add 4 is 11, what is the answer to 11 subtract 4? What about 110 subtract 40? What about 1·1 subtract 0·4?*

 Pairs

- Provide each pair with a copy of the *Facts and Games: Years 5 & 6* book and direct their attention to the two tables on pages 13 and 14, the two tables on pages 15 and 16 or the two tables on pages 17 and 18.
- Children spend just two or three minutes individually looking at the table(s) with the aim of developing greater fluency of the facts.
- Children then take turns to ask each other questions similar to the following:
  - *Show me how to find the answer to 0·6 add 0·3.*
  - *What is the answer to 0·08 subtract 0·05? Show me this answer on the table.*
  - *Show me how to find the answer to 230 subtract 70.*
  - *What is the answer to 210 subtract 30?*

Individual

- Provide each child with a copy of the *Facts and Games: Years 5 & 6* book and direct their attention to the two tables on pages 13 and 14, the two tables on pages 15 and 16 or the two tables on pages 17 and 18.
- It is recommended that the child spends just five or ten minutes each time, focussing their attention on developing greater fluency of the facts.
- To provide some personal challenge, suggest the child covers the answers on the table leaving only the numbers in the top row and left-hand column visible. The child tests themselves on the addition number facts to 20 and the addition of 1-digit and 2-digit numbers to 20 (pages 13 and 14), the multiples of 10 from 10 to 200 (pages 15 and 16) or decimals involving tenths or hundredths (pages 17 and 18).

Animal range

Addition

Subtraction

Objective

- Add and subtract mentally two 2-digit numbers

Pupil resources

- *Fluency in Number Facts: Facts and Games: Years 5 & 6* book pages 56 and 57 (per pair); PDFs:

- 2 × 0–9 dice (per pair)
- 12 counters: 6 of one colour, 6 of another colour for 'Animal range – Addition' (per pair)
- 10 counters: 5 of one colour, 5 of another colour for 'Animal range – Subtraction' (per pair)

Variations

Animal range – Addition

- Children play the game in groups of three. You need 18 counters: six each of three different colours.

- Children play the games individually. If they can't place a counter on a turn, discard one of the 12 counters.

  Golden rule: Only one counter can go on each animal. How few goes does it take to place six counters on the animals?

Animal range – Subtraction

- Children play the game in groups of three. You need 15 counters: 5 each of 3 different colours.

- Children play the games individually. If they can't place a counter on a turn, discard one of the 10 counters.

  Golden rule: Only one counter can go on each animal. How few goes does it take to place five counters on the animals?

Animal range – Addition and Subtraction

or   Each player needs two 0–9 dice and six counters all the same colour. Players must have different coloured counters. Each player places one of their counters on an animal and rolls their two dice to make a 2-digit number. They then decide whether to add or subtract their dice number to or from a number within the range of their animal's numbers. The player with the answer nearest 100 wins that round and leaves their counter on the animal. The other players remove their counters from the animals. The winner is the first player to have one of their counters on six different animals.

Roman additions

Objective

- Add mentally multiples of 100 and 1000

Pupil resources

- *Fluency in Number Facts: Facts and Games:*
  Years 5 & 6 book pages 58 and 59 (per pair); PDFs:

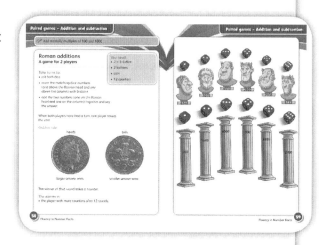

Paired games
and activities

Paired games
from the *Facts and
Games: Years 5 &
6 book*

- 2 × 1–6 dice (per pair)
- 2 buttons (per pair)
- coin (per pair)
- 12 counters (per pair)

Variations

- Children play the game in groups of three. On coin toss: heads = largest number wins; tails = smallest number wins.

 or

Subtract mentally multiples of 100 and 1000

- Children subtract the number on the column from the number on the Roman head. When placing the buttons, ensure that the number on the Roman head is larger than the number on the column, i.e. if 4 and 6 are rolled on the dice, put the buttons on numbers 5372 (Roman head 6) and 800 (column 4), not 2802 (Roman head 4) and 5200 (column 6). If playing the game in groups, on the coin toss: heads = largest number wins; tails = smallest number wins.

Helicopters and buses

Objective

- Subtract mentally multiples of 100 and 1000

Pupil resources

- *Fluency in Number Facts: Facts and Games: Years 5 & 6* book pages 60 and 61 (per pair); PDFs:

Paired games and activities → Paired games from the *Facts and Games: Years 5 & 6* book

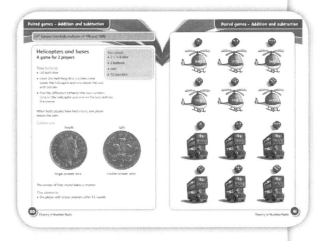

- 2 × 1–6 dice (per pair)
- 2 buttons (per pair)
- coin (per pair)
- 12 counters (per pair)

Variations

- Children play the game in groups of three. On coin toss: heads = largest number wins; tails = smallest number wins.

  or

Add mentally multiples of 100 and 1000

- Children add the number on the bus to the number on the helicopter. If playing the game in groups, on coin toss: heads = largest number wins; tails = smallest number wins.

Sunflower sums

Addition

Subtraction

Objective

- Add and subtract mentally a 2-digit number to or from a 3-digit number

Pupil resources

- *Fluency in Number Facts: Facts and Games: Years 5 & 6* book pages 62 and 63 (per pair); PDFs:

Paired games and activities → Paired games from the *Facts and Games: Years 5 & 6 book*

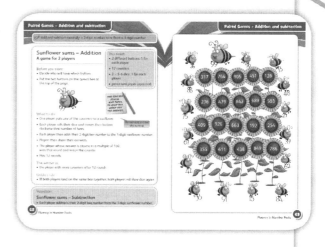

- 2 different buttons: 1 for each player (per pair)
- 12 counters (per pair)
- 2 × 1–6 dice: 1 for each player (per pair)
- pencil and paper – optional (per pair)

Variations

- Children play both games in groups of three. You need three different buttons and three 1–6 dice: one for each player.

Sunflower sums – Addition

 or

- Children use the 12 counters, but just one button and one dice. They begin by putting the button on the queen bee. One player then puts a counter on a flower. Another player rolls the dice and moves the button clockwise that number of bees. Each player then adds the bee number to the flower number. The first player to say the correct answer takes the counter. The winner is the player with more counters after 12 rounds.

Sunflower sums – Subtraction

 or

- Play the game as described above. Each player subtracts the bee number from the flower number.

Explorer's map

Addition
subtraction

Objective

- Add and subtract decimals mentally: U·t ± U·t

Pupil resources

- *Fluency in Number Facts: Facts and Games: Years 5 & 6* book pages 64 and 65 (per pair); PDFs:

Paired games
and activities

Paired games from
the *Facts and Games:
Years 5 & 6* book

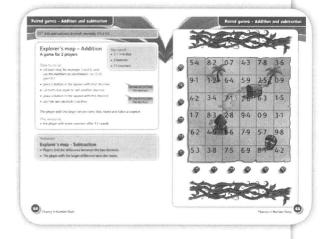

- 2 × 1–6 dice (per pair)
- 2 buttons (per pair)
- 12 counters (per pair)

Variations

- Children play both games in groups of three.
  - **Explorer's map – Addition**

    The player with the largest answers wins the round and takes a counter.
  - **Explorer's map – Subtraction**

    The player with the largest difference wins the round and takes a counter.

Explorer's map – Addition

- Do not use the dice or buttons. Use 36 counters. Cover all the decimals with a counter. Each player removes one counter. Both players add the two decimals together. The first player to say the correct answer takes both counters. The game continues until all 36 counters are removed from the map. The winner is the player with more counters.

Explorer's map – Subtraction

- Play the game as described above. Both players find the difference between the two decimals.

Fishing for 1

Objective

- Add and subtract decimals mentally, including calculating complements of 1, e.g. 0·83 + 0·17

Pupil resources

- *Fluency in Number Facts: Facts and Games: Years 5 & 6* book pages 66 and 67 (per pair); PDFs:

 → Paired games and activities → Paired games from the *Facts and Games: Years 5 & 6* book

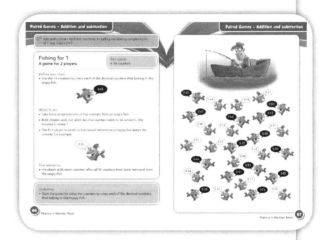

- 14 counters (per pair)

Variations

- Children play the game in groups of three.

Add decimals mentally: U·th + U·th
- You need 28 counters. Cover all the decimals with a counter. Each player removes one counter. Both players add the two decimals together. The first player to say the correct answer takes both counters. The game continues until all 28 counters are removed from the fish. The winner is the player with more counters.

Subtract decimals mentally: U·th – U·th
- Play the game as described above. Both players find the difference between the two decimals.

Addition and Subtraction Flip Facts cards

Objective

- Recall addition and subtraction facts to 20 fluently

Resources

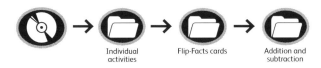

Individual activities → Flip-Facts cards → Addition and subtraction

- 'Addition and subtraction Flip Facts cards'
- scissors
- glue
- hole punch
- small piece of string or paper fastener

What to do

- Cut out the cards along the dashed lines.
- Fold each card along the dotted lines to form two-sided cards.
- Glue together the back of each card.
- Punch a hole in the centre of each card.
- Arrange the cards in order with the smallest number on top.
- Fasten the set of cards together with string or a paper fastener.

To practise the addition facts for 12

- Use the 'Addition and subtraction Flip Facts cards for 12'.
- Start with the 0 card on top.
- Ask yourself: *0, how many more to make 12?* (12) Turn over the card to check. *1, how many more to make 12?* (11) Turn over the card to check. *2, how many more to make 12?* (10) Turn over the card to check.
- Continue until you reach the card showing 6 and once again ask: *6, how many more to make 12?* (6).
- Now turn the pack of cards around asking: *6, how many more to make 12?* (6). Turn over the card to check. *7, how many more to make 12?* (5). Turn over the card to check. *8, how many more to make 12?* (4) and so on.
- Repeat several times, quickening the pace as you go.

(continued)

Addition and subtraction facts

To practise the subtraction facts for 12

- Use the 'Addition and subtraction Flip Facts cards for 12'.
- Start with the 0 card on top.
- Ask yourself: *12 take away 0 is?* (12). Turn over the card to check. *12 take away 1 is?* (11). Turn over the card to check. *12 take away 2 is?* (10). Turn over the card to check.
- Continue until you reach the card showing 6 and once again ask: *12 take away 6 is?* (6).
- Now turn the pack of cards around asking: *12 take away 6 is?* (6). Turn over the card to check. *12 take away 7 is?* (5). Turn over the card to check. *12 take away 8 is?* (4) and so on.
- Repeat several times, quickening the pace as you go.

- Children spend just five or ten minutes each time, focussing their attention on learning the addition and subtraction facts off by heart.

Variation

- Use other sets of flip facts cards to practise the addition and subtraction facts for 1–11, 13–20.

Hold it up

Objectives

- Recall and use multiplication and division facts for multiplication tables up to 12 × 12
- Multiply and divide numbers mentally drawing upon known facts
- Multiply and divide whole numbers and those involving decimals by 10, 100 and 1000

Teacher resources

Whole-class games and activities → PowerPoint slides

- 'Hold it up'

Pupil resources

- set of 0–9 number cards or small individual whiteboard and pen (per child)

What to do

- Using either the 'Hold it up: Numbers 1–10' slide or 'Hold it up: Numbers 1–12' slide, in the box at the top of the slide write the multiplication symbol and multiplication table you want the children to practise and consolidate, for example, × 4.
- Point to one of the coloured 1–10 or 1–12 numbers on the slide.
- Children work out the answer and hold up the appropriate number card(s), for example, 4 × 3 = 12, so the children should hold up a 1 and a 2 number card to show '12'; or children can write the answer on the whiteboard.
- Repeat several times.

Variations

- Use the 'Hold it up: Numbers 1–20' or 'Hold it up: 2-digit numbers' slide.
- Use the 'Hold it up: Numbers 1–12', 'Hold it up: Numbers 1–20', 'Hold it up: 2-digit numbers' or 'Hold it up: 3-digit numbers' slide and write ÷ 10, ÷ 100 or ÷ 1000 in the box at the top of the slide.
- Use the 'Hold it up: Numbers 1–12' slide and write a multiple of 10 or 100, for example, × 40 or × 600 in the box at the top of the slide.
- Use the 'Hold it up: Numbers 1–12', slide and write a decimal from × 0·2 to × 1·2 in the box at the top of the slide.
- Use the 'Hold it up: Tenths' slide and write a multiple of × 10, × 100, × 1000 in the box at the top of the slide.
- Use the 'Hold it up: Tenths' slide and write × 10, × 100, × 1000, ÷ 10 or ÷ 100 in the box at the top of the slide.
- Use the 'Hold it up: Hundredths' slide and write × 10, × 100, × 1000 or ÷ 10 in the box at the top of the slide.
- Use the 'Hold it up: Thousandths' slide and write × 10, × 100, × 1000 in the box at the top of the slide.
- Use the 11 'Hold it up' times tables slides to practise the division facts for multiplication tables up to 12 × 12.

Around the clock

Objectives

- Recall and use multiplication and division facts for multiplication tables up to 12 × 12
- Multiply and divide numbers mentally drawing upon known facts

Teacher resources

Whole-class games and activities → PowerPoint slides

- 'Around the clock'

Pupil resources

Number cards

Around the clock

Fluency in Number Facts Years 5 & 6   www.collinseducation.com © HarperCollinsPublishers Limited 2013

- set of 'Multiples of…number cards' or small individual whiteboard and pen (per child)

What to do

- Using the 'Around the clock' slide, on the circle in the centre of the clock write the multiplication table you want the children to practise and consolidate, for example, × 4.
- Provide each child with the corresponding set of 'Multiples of…number cards' or an individual whiteboard and pen.
- Point to one of the 1–12 numbers on the clock face.
- Children work out the answer and hold up the appropriate multiples card or write the answer on the whiteboard.
- Repeat several times.

Variations

- Provide pairs of children with a set of multiples cards, and tell the children to work together.
- *Don't* write the multiplication table on the circle in the centre of the clock and don't provide the children with the multiples number cards. Point to one of the 1–12 numbers on the clock face, say *times 2, times 3…* or *times 12*. Children work out the answer and put up their hand or write the answer on the whiteboard.
- Write a multiple of 10 or 100, for example, × 80 or × 300 in the circle.
- Write a decimal in the circle, for example, × 0·2, × 0·6 or × 0·9.
- Draw children's attention to the small, unlabelled divisions around the clock face. Explain that each division is halfway between two numbers. If you point to one of these divisions, for example, between 6 and 7, that this division represents 6·5 and needs to be multiplied by the number in the centre of the circle.

Gladiators

Objectives

- Recall and use multiplication and division facts for multiplication tables up to 12 × 12
- Multiply and divide numbers mentally drawing upon known facts
- Multiply and divide whole numbers and those involving decimals by 10, 100 and 1000

Teacher resources

Whole-class games and activities → PowerPoint slides

- 'Gladiators'

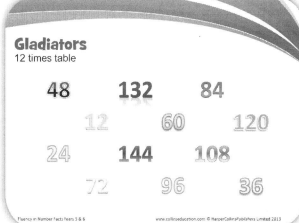

Gladiators
12 times table

48	132	84
12	60	120
24	144	108
72	96	36

Fluency in Number Facts Years 5 & 6   www.collinseducation.com © HarperCollinsPublishers Limited 2013

Pupil resources

- 2 × rulers or 'swords'

What to do

- Decide which multiplication table you want the children to practise and consolidate and display the appropriate 'Gladiators' times-table slide.
- Ask two children to stand either side of the numbers.
- Ask a multiplication fact for the corresponding multiplication table, for example: *Six multiplied by nine is…*
- The first child to point to the correct answer stays in. The other child sits down.
- Quickly choose another child to come and take the place of the child that just sat down.
- Continue as above.
- Which child can stay in the longest?

Variations

- The children sitting down ask the two children standing by the numbers a question where the answer is on the slide.
- To quicken the game, have two children standing either side of the numbers, one behind the other. When a child loses and has to sit down, there is an immediate replacement.
- Use the other 'Gladiators: Times tables' slides and the 'Gladiators: Division facts' slide.
- Use the 'Gladiators: Multiples of 20 / 30 / 40 / 50 / 60 / 70 / 80 / 90 / 100 / 110 or 120' game board to ask questions involving multiples of 10 that are related to a specific multiplication table.
- Use the 'Gladiators: Multiples of 10 and 100' and 'Gladiators: Multiples of 100 and 1000' slides to ask questions involving multiplying and dividing multiples of 10, 100 and 1000 by numbers 1 to 12 and multiplying pairs of multiples of 10 and 100.
- Use the 'Gladiators: Multiples of 0·2 / 0·3 / 0·4 / 0·5 / 0·6 / 0·7 / 0·8 / 0·9 / 1·1 or 1·2' slide to ask questions involving decimals that are related to a specific multiplication table.
- Use the 'Gladiators: Tenths' slide to ask questions related to multiplication facts involving decimals, for example, 0·8 × 7.
- Use the 'Gladiators: Tenths' and 'Gladiators: Hundredths' slides to ask questions related to multiplying and dividing whole numbers and decimals by 10, 100 and 1000.
- Use the 'Gladiators: Division facts (decimals)' slide to ask questions related to division facts involving decimals, for example, 4·8 ÷ 6.

Hands-on

Objectives

- Recall and use multiplication and division facts for multiplication tables up to 12 × 12
- Multiply and divide numbers mentally drawing upon known facts
- Multiply and divide whole numbers and those involving decimals by 10, 100 and 1000

Teacher resources

- none

Pupil resources

Whole-class games and activities → PowerPoint slides

- 'Hands-on' game board (per pair)

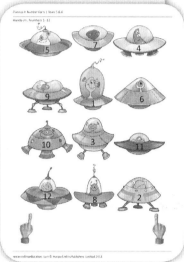

What to do

- Decide which multiplication table you want the children to practise and consolidate. If practising the multiplication facts for one of the multiplication tables up to 12 × 12, use the corresponding 'Hands-on: Multiples of... 'game board. If practising the division facts for one of the multiplication tables up to 12 × 12 use the 'Hands-on: Numbers 1–12' game board.
- Arrange the children into pairs and provide each pair with a copy of the appropriate 'Hands-on' game board.
- Tell the children to put the game board between them and each child to put their index finger on a hand at the bottom of the game board.
- Ask an appropriate multiplication or division fact for the multiplication table the children are practising, for example: *Seven times nine* (if practising the multiplication facts for the 9 multiplication table) or *54 divided by nine* (if practising the division facts for the 9 multiplication table).
- The first child to point to the correct answer wins.
- Children keep count of how many games they win.
- Play for as long as is appropriate.
- The winner in each pair is the child who wins more rounds.

Variations

- Provide each pair with a pile of counters. As a child wins a game they take a counter. The winner in each pair is the child who wins more counters.
- Use the 'Hands-on: Multiples of 20 / 30 / 40 / 50 / 60 / 70 / 80 / 90 / 100 / 110 or 120' game board to ask questions involving multiples of 10 that are related to a specific multiplication table.
- Use the 'Hands-on: 2- and 3-digit multiples of 10' game board to ask questions involving multiplying and dividing multiples of 10 by numbers 1 to 12.
- Use the 'Hands-on: Multiples of 0·2 / 0·3 / 0·4 / 0·5 / 0·6 / 0·7 / 0·8 / 0·9 / 1·1 or 1·2' game board to ask questions involving decimals that are related to a specific multiplication table.
- Use the 'Hands-on: Tenths' game board to ask questions related to multiplication facts involving decimals, for example, 0·4 × 6, and dividing whole numbers by 10.
- Use the 'Hands-on: 0·1–1·2' game board to ask questions related to division facts involving decimals, for example, 4·8 ÷ 6.

Objectives

- Recall and use multiplication and division facts for multiplication tables up to 12 × 12
- Multiply and divide numbers mentally drawing upon known facts
- Multiply and divide whole numbers and those involving decimals by 10, 100 and 1000

Teacher resources

CD → Whole-class games and activities → PowerPoint slides

- 'Bingo'

Pupil resources

- pencil and paper or small individual whiteboard and pen (per child)

Bingo
12 × 12 multiplication tables

4	9	50	14	64	40	20	144	108	72
100	63	66	88	15	99	49	11	48	3
33	10	24	1	30	55	21	18	120	96
60	7	6	35	12	28	132	90	70	16
25	2	42	44	84	81	22	80	5	77
	27	56	54	36	8	110	45	32	

Fluency in Number Facts Years 5 & 6   www.collinseducation.com © HarperCollinsPublishers Limited 2013

What to do

- Display the 'Bingo: 12 × 12 multiplication tables' slide.
- Ask each child to write down any five numbers from the slide.
- Ask questions involving the multiplication and division facts for multiplication tables up to 12 × 12.
- Children look to find if any of their five numbers is the answer to the question.
- If a child has the answer, they cross out that number.
- The winner is the first child to cross out all five of their numbers and call out 'Bingo!'

(**Note:** Be sure to keep a record of the answers for checking purposes.)

Variations

- Ask the children to write down more or fewer than five numbers from the slide.
- Use the 'Bingo: Multiples of 10 and 100' and 'Bingo: Multiples of 100 and 1000' slide to ask questions involving multiplying and dividing multiples of 10, 100 and 1000 by numbers 1 to 12 and multiplying pairs of multiples of 10 and 100.
- Use the 'Bingo: Tenths' slide to ask questions related to multiplication facts involving decimals, for example, 0·8 × 7.
- Use the 'Bingo: Tenths' and 'Bingo: Hundredths' slides to ask questions related to multiplying and dividing whole numbers and decimals by 10, 100 and 1000.

Four in a row

Objectives

- Recall and use multiplication facts for multiplication tables up to 12 × 12
- Multiply numbers mentally drawing upon known facts

Teacher resources

Whole-class games and activities → PowerPoint slides

- 'Four in a row'
- 1–12 dice

Pupil resources

- none

Four in a row
12 × 12 multiplication tables

50	36	77	30	80	54	70	11	35	9
27	32	12	110	21	144	48	16	108	18
8	66	72	10	88	64	6	81	45	120
24	100	3	132	96	9	33	40	20	5
14	42	60	84	25	2	56	55	90	63
22	99	121	15	44	49	24	28	4	7

Fluency in Number Facts Years 5 & 6   www.collinseducation.com © HarperCollins Publishers Limited 2013

What to do

- Divide the class into two teams – a red team and a blue team.
- Display the 'Four in a row: 12 × 12 multiplication tables' slide.
- Explain that the object of the game is for a team to highlight a row of four numbers either side to side, up and down or diagonally.
- To highlight a number, a team must successfully answer a multiplication fact for the multiplication tables up to 12 × 12.
- Invite a child from the red team to roll the dice and say the number, for example, 6.
- Decide whether to multiply the dice number by 2, 3, 4, 5, 6, 7, 8, 9, 10, 11 or 12 and say the corresponding calculation, for example: *6 multiplied by 9*.
- Select a child from the red team to call out the answer.
- If correct, this number is highlighted in red on the slide. If incorrect, ask a child from the blue team to give the answer. If correct, this number is highlighted in blue.
- Next, invite a child from the blue team to roll the dice.
- Repeat the above, at a quick pace, until one team has highlighted a row of four numbers.

Variations

- Use the 'Four in a row: 2- and 3-digit multiples of 10' slide and decide whether to multiply the dice number by 20, 30, 40, 50, 60, 70, 80, 90, 100, 110 or 120, making sure that the product is on the slide.
- Use the 'Four in a row: Tenths' slide and decide whether to multiply the dice number by 0·2, 0·3, 0·4, 0·5, 0·6, 0·7, 0·8, 0·9, 1, 1·1 or 1·2, making sure that the product is on the slide.
- The team that rolls the dice decides whether to multiply the dice number by 2, 3, 4, 5, 6, 7, 8, 9, 10, 11 or 12.

Objectives

- Recall and use multiplication and division facts for multiplication tables up to 12 × 12
- Multiply and divide numbers mentally drawing upon known facts

Teacher resources

⊙ → 📁 → 📁

Whole-class games and activities PowerPoint slides

- 'Tell me the facts'

Pupil resources

- none

Tell me the facts

Multiplication

4	7	3	9	4	11
9	2	6	11	3	9
6	8	7	2	7	10
3	5	4	10	8	7
10	11	8	5	6	3
12	2	5	12	9	12

Fluency in Number Facts Years 5 & 6   www.collinseducation.com © HarperCollinsPublishers Limited 2013

What to do

- Display the 'Tell me the facts: Multiplication' slide.
- Ask a child to highlight two numbers next to each other either side to side, up and down, or diagonally and say a known multiplication number fact about these two numbers, i.e. *I know that the product of 8 and 7 is 56.*
- Repeat, asking other children to come and highlight two other numbers, saying a known multiplication fact about the two numbers.

Variations

- Use the 'Tell me the facts: Multiplication (decimals)' slide, asking questions such as: *Point to two numbers next to each other that have a product of 6·4.*
- Use the 'Tell me the facts: 12 × 12 division' slide, asking questions such as: *Point to two numbers next to each other that give an answer of 7 when the larger number is divided by the smaller number.*

Multiplication and division facts

Who's left standing?

Objectives

- Recall and use multiplication and division facts for multiplication tables up to 12 × 12
- Multiply and divide numbers mentally drawing upon known facts

Teacher resources

- none

Pupil resources

- '1–12 number cards' or 'Multiples of…number cards' (one card per child)

What to do

Decide which multiplication table you want the children to practise and consolidate:

- If practising the multiplication facts for one of the multiplication tables up to 12 × 12, use the corresponding 'Multiples of 2 / 3 / 4 / 5 / 6 / 7 / 8 / 9 / 10 / 11 / 12 number cards'.
- If practising the multiplication facts for one of the multiplication tables involving multiples of 10, use the corresponding 'Multiples of 20 / 30 / 40 / 50 / 60 / 70 / 80 / 90 / 100 / 110 / 120 number cards'.
- If practising the multiplication facts for one of the multiplication tables involving decimals, use the corresponding 'Multiples of 0·2 / 0·3 / 0·4 / 0·5 / 0·6 / 0·7 / 0·8 / 0·9 / (1–12 number cards), / 1·1 / 1·2 number cards'.
- If practising the division facts for one of the multiplication tables up to 12 × 12, use the '1–12 number cards'.
- If practising the division facts for one of the multiplication tables involving multiples of 10, use the 'Multiples of 10 number cards'.
- If practising the division facts for one of the multiplication tables involving decimals, use the '0·1 to 1·2 number cards'.

For the 2 multiplication table

To recall the multiplication facts for the 2 multiplication table:
- Provide each child with a 'Multiples of 2 number card'.
- Say: *Everyone stand up. Look at the number on your card. Sit down if the number on your card is the answer to:*
  - *4 multiplied by 2 (8)*
  - *12 times 2 (24)*
  - *6 multiplied by 2 (12)*
  - *2 multiplied by 2 (4)*
  - *the product of 9 and 2 (18)*
  - *10 times 2 (20)*
  - *8 times 2 (16)*
  - *7 multiplied by 2 (14)*
  - *11 multiplied by 2 (22)*
  - *1 times 2 (2)*
  - *the product of 3 and 2 (6)*

The winners are the children still standing with 10 on their cards.

To use the multiplication facts for the 2 multiplication table to recall related facts involving multiples of 10, adapt the game above. Provide each child with a 'Multiples of 20 number card'. Say: *Everyone stand up….Sit down if the number on your card is the answer to 4 multiplied by 20. (80)*

Who's left standing?

(continued)

To use the multiplication facts for the 2 multiplication table to recall related facts involving decimals adapt the game above. Provide each child with a 'Multiples of 0·2 number card'. Say: *Everyone stand up…Sit down if the number on your card is the answer to 4 multiplied by 0·2. (0·8)*

To recall the division facts for the 2 multiplication table:

- Provide each child with a '1–12 number card'.

- Say: *Everyone stand up. Look at the number on your card. Sit down if the number on your card is the answer to:*

  - *2 divided into 12 (6)*
  - *22 divided by 2 (11)*
  - *24 divided by 2 (12)*
  - *2 divided into 18 (9)*
  - *8 divided by 2 (4)*
  - *20 divided by 2 (10)*
  - *10 divided by 2 (5)*
  - *2 divided into 6 (3)*
  - *2 divided by 2 (1)*
  - *2 divided into 14 (7)*
  - *16 divided by 2 (8)*

The winners are the children still standing with 2 on their cards.

To use the division facts for the 2 multiplication table to recall related facts involving multiples of 20, adapt the game above. Provide each child with a 'Multiples of 10 number card'. Say: *Everyone stand up…Sit down if the number on your card is the answer to 2 divided into 120. (60)*

To use the division facts for the 2 multiplication table to recall related facts involving decimals, adapt the game above. Provide each child with a '0·1–1·2 number card'. Say: *Everyone stand up…Sit down if the number on your card is the answer to 2 divided into 1·2. (0·6)*

For the 3 multiplication table

To recall the multiplication facts for the 3 multiplication table:

- Provide each child with a 'Multiples of 3 number card'.

- Say: *Everyone stand up. Look at the number on your card. Sit down if the number on your card is the answer to:*

  - *3 multiplied by 3 (9)*
  - *7 times 3 (21)*
  - *12 multiplied by 3 (36)*
  - *8 times 3 (24)*
  - *5 times 3 (15)*
  - *1 multiplied by 3 (3)*
  - *4 multiplied by 3 (12)*
  - *2 times 3 (6)*
  - *the product of 11 and 3 (33)*
  - *9 multiplied by 3 (27)*
  - *the product of 10 and 3 (30)*

The winners are the children still standing with 18 on their cards.

To use the multiplication facts for the 3 multiplication table to recall related facts involving multiples of 10, adapt the game above. Provide each child with a 'Multiples of 30 number card'. Say: *Everyone stand up…Sit down if the number on your card is the answer to 3 multiplied by 30. (90)*

To use the multiplication facts for the 3 multiplication table to recall related facts involving decimals, adapt the game above. Provide each child with a 'Multiples of 0·3 number card'. Say: *Everyone stand up…Sit down if the number on your card is the answer to 3 multiplied by 0·3. (0·9)*

(continued)

Who's left standing?

(continued)

To recall the division facts for the 3 multiplication table:

- Provide each child with a '1–12 number card'.
- Say: *Everyone stand up. Look at the number on your card. Sit down if the number on your card is the answer to:*
  - – *36 divided by 3* (12)
  - – *3 divided into 27* (9)
  - – *15 divided by 3* (5)
  - – *3 divided into 6* (2)
  - – *12 divided by 3* (4)
  - – *3 divided into 21* (7)
  - – *24 divided by 3* (8)
  - – *3 divided by 3* (1)
  - – *33 divided by 3* (11)
  - – *3 divided into 18* (6)
  - – *9 divided by 3* (3)

The winners are the children still standing with 10 on their cards.

To use the division facts for the 3 multiplication table to recall related facts involving multiples of 30, adapt the game above. Provide each child with a 'Multiples of 10 number card'. Say: *Everyone stand up…Sit down if the number on your card is the answer to 360 divided by 3.* (120)

To use the division facts for the 3 multiplication table to recall related facts involving decimals, adapt the game above. Provide each child with a '0·1–1·2 number card'. Say: *Everyone stand up…Sit down if the number on your card is the answer to 3·6 divided by 3.* (1·2)

For the 4 multiplication table

To recall the multiplication facts for the 4 multiplication table:

- Provide each child with a 'Multiples of 4 number card'.
- Say: *Everyone stand up. Look at the number on your card. Sit down if the number on your card is the answer to:*
  - – *5 times 4* (20)
  - – *7 times 4* (28)
  - – *1 multiplied by 4* (4)
  - – *11 times 4* (44)
  - – *2 times 4* (8)
  - – *the product of 9 and 4* (36)
  - – *12 multiplied by 4* (48)
  - – *8 times 4* (32)
  - – *4 multiplied by 4* (16)
  - – *6 multiplied by 4* (24)
  - – *the product of 3 and 4* (12)

The winners are the children still standing with 40 on their cards.

To use the multiplication facts for the 4 multiplication table to recall related facts involving multiples of 10, adapt the game above. Provide each child with a 'Multiples of 40 number card'. Say: *Everyone stand up…Sit down if the number on your card is the answer to 5 times 40.* (200)

To use the multiplication facts for the 4 multiplication table to recall related facts involving decimals, adapt the game above. Provide each child with a 'Multiples of 0·4 number card'. Say: *Everyone stand up…Sit down if the number on your card is the answer to 5 times 0·4.* (2)

Who's left standing?

(continued)

To recall the division facts for the 4 multiplication table:

- Provide each child with a '1–12 number card'.
- Say: *Everyone stand up. Look at the number on your card. Sit down if the number on your card is the answer to:*
  - – *4 divided into 24 (6)*
  - – *20 divided by 4 (5)*
  - – *48 divided by 4 (12)*
  - – *4 divided into 36 (9)*
  - – *16 divided by 4 (4)*
  - – *40 divided by 4 (10)*
  - – *12 divided by 4 (3)*
  - – *4 divided into 8 (2)*
  - – *4 divided by 4 (1)*
  - – *44 divided by 4 (11)*
  - – *4 divided into 32 (8)*

The winners are the children still standing with 7 on their cards.

To use the division facts for the 4 multiplication table to recall related facts involving multiples of 40, adapt the game above. Provide each child with a 'Multiples of 10 number card'. Say: *Everyone stand up…Sit down if the number on your card is the answer to 4 divided into 240. (60)*

To use the division facts for the 4 multiplication table to recall related facts involving decimals, adapt the game above. Provide each child with a '0·1–1·2 number card'. Say: *Everyone stand up…Sit down if the number on your card is the answer to 4 divided into 2·4. (0·6)*

For the 5 multiplication table

To recall the multiplication facts for the 5 multiplication table:

- Provide each child with a 'Multiples of 5 number card'.
- Say: *Everyone stand up. Look at the number on your card. Sit down if the number on your card is the answer to:*
  - – *6 times 5 (30)*
  - – *11 multiplied by 5 (55)*
  - – *1 times 5 (5)*
  - – *the product of 8 and 5 (40)*
  - – *5 multiplied by 5 (25)*
  - – *the product of 7 and 5 (35)*
  - – *2 multiplied by 5 (10)*
  - – *10 times 5 (50)*
  - – *the product of 3 and 5 (15)*
  - – *9 multiplied by 5 (45)*
  - – *4 times 5 (20)*

The winners are the children still standing with 60 on their cards.

To use the multiplication facts for the 5 multiplication table to recall related facts involving multiples of 10, adapt the game above. Provide each child with a 'Multiples of 50 number card'. Say: *Everyone stand up…Sit down if the number on your card is the answer to 6 times 50. (300)*

To use the multiplication facts for the 5 multiplication table to recall related facts involving decimals, adapt the game above. Provide each child with a 'Multiples of 0·5 number card'. Say: *Everyone stand up…Sit down if the number on your card is the answer to 6 times 0·5. (3)*

(continued)

Who's left standing?

(continued)

To recall the division facts for the 5 multiplication table:

- Provide each child with a '1–12 number card'.
- Say: *Everyone stand up. Look at the number on your card. Sit down if the number on your card is the answer to:*
  - *55 divided by 5* (11)
  - *50 divided by 5* (10)
  - *30 divided by 5* (6)
  - *5 divided into 25* (5)
  - *5 divided into 35* (7)
  - *40 divided by 5* (8)
  - *5 divided into 10* (2)
  - *20 divided by 5* (4)
  - *5 divided into 45* (9)
  - *5 divided by 5* (1)
  - *60 divided by 5* (12)

The winners are the children still standing with 3 on their cards.

To use the division facts for the 5 multiplication table to recall related facts involving multiples of 50, adapt the game above. Provide each child with a 'Multiples of 10 number card'. Say: *Everyone stand up…Sit down if the number on your card is the answer to 550 divided by 5.* (110)

To use the division facts for the 5 multiplication table to recall related facts involving decimals, adapt the game above. Provide each child with a '0·1 to 1·2 number card'. Say: *Everyone stand up…Sit down if the number on your card is the answer to 5·5 divided by 5.* (1·1)

For the 6 multiplication table

To recall the multiplication facts for the 6 multiplication table:

- Provide each child with a 'Multiples of 6 number card'.
- Say: *Everyone stand up. Look at the number on your card. Sit down if the number on your card is the answer to:*
  - *3 times 6* (18)
  - *5 multiplied by 6* (30)
  - *11 times 6* (66)
  - *the product of 12 and 6* (72)
  - *10 times 6* (60)
  - *6 multiplied by 6* (36)
  - *1 multiplied by 6* (6)
  - *7 times 6* (42)
  - *the product of 2 and 6* (12)
  - *4 multiplied by 6* (24)
  - *the product of 8 and 6* (48)

The winners are the children still standing with 54 on their cards.

To use the multiplication facts for the 6 multiplication table to recall related facts involving multiples of 10, adapt the game above. Provide each child with a 'Multiples of 60 number card'. Say: *Everyone stand up…Sit down if the number on your card is the answer to 3 times 60.* (180)

To use the multiplication facts for the 6 multiplication table to recall related facts involving decimals, adapt the game above. Provide each child with a 'Multiples of 0·6 number card'. Say: *Everyone stand up…Sit down if the number on your card is the answer to 3 times 0·6.* (1·8)

Who's left standing?

(continued)

To recall the division facts for the 6 multiplication table:

- Provide each child with a '1–12 number card'.
- Say: *Everyone stand up. Look at the number on your card. Sit down if the number on your card is the answer to:*
  - *66 divided by 6* (11)
  - *42 divided by 6* (7)
  - *60 divided by 6* (10)
  - *72 divided by 6* (12)
  - *36 divided by 6* (6)
  - *6 divided into 18* (3)
  - *6 divided into 30* (5)
  - *6 divided into 54* (9)
  - *6 divided by 6* (1)
  - *48 divided by 6* (8)
  - *6 divided into 24* (4)

The winners are the children still standing with 2 on their cards.

To use the division facts for the 6 multiplication table to recall related facts involving multiples of 60, adapt the game above. Provide each child with a 'Multiples of 10 number card'. Say: *Everyone stand up…Sit down if the number on your card is the answer to 660 divided by 6.* (110)

To use the division facts for the 6 multiplication table to recall related facts involving decimals, adapt the game above. Provide each child with a '0·1–1·2 number card'. Say: *Everyone stand up. …Sit down if the number on your card is the answer to 6·6 divided by 6.* (1·1)

For the 7 multiplication table

To recall the multiplication facts for the 7 multiplication table:

- Provide each child with a 'Multiples of 7 number card'.
- Say: *Everyone stand up. Look at the number on your card. Sit down if the number on your card is the answer to:*
  - *6 times 7* (42)
  - *4 multiplied by 7* (28)
  - *10 times 7* (70)
  - *11 times 7* (77)
  - *the product of 3 and 7* (21)
  - *8 multiplied by 7* (56)
  - *9 times 7* (63)
  - *the product of 5 and 7* (35)
  - *7 multiplied by 7* (49)
  - *12 multiplied by 7* (84)
  - *the product of 2 and 7* (14)

The winners are the children still standing with 7 on their cards.

To use the multiplication facts for the 7 multiplication table to recall related facts involving multiples of 10, adapt the game above. Provide each child with a 'Multiples of 70 number card'. Say: *Everyone stand up…Sit down if the number on your card is the answer to 6 times 70.* (420)

To use the multiplication facts for the 7 multiplication table to recall related facts involving decimals, adapt the game above. Provide each child with a 'Multiples of 0·7 number card'. Say: *Everyone stand up…Sit down if the number on your card is the answer to 6 times 0·7.* (4·2)

(continued)

Who's left standing?

(continued)

To recall the division facts for the 7 multiplication table:

- Provide each child with a '1–12 number card'.
- Say: *Everyone stand up. Look at the number on your card. Sit down if the number on your card is the answer to:*
  - *7 divided by 7 (1)*
  - *7 divided into 21 (3)*
  - *70 divided by 7 (10)*
  - *84 divided by 7 (12)*
  - *42 divided by 7 (6)*
  - *7 divided into 35 (5)*
  - *49 divided by 7 (7)*
  - *7 divided into 63 (9)*
  - *28 divided by 7 (4)*
  - *7 divided into 14 (2)*
  - *56 divided by 7 (8)*

The winners are the children still standing with 11 on their cards.

To use the division facts for the 7 multiplication table to recall related facts involving multiples of 70, adapt the game above. Provide each child with a 'Multiples of 10 number card'. Say: *Everyone stand up…Sit down if the number on your card is the answer to 70 divided by 7. (10)*

To use the division facts for the 7 multiplication table to recall related facts involving decimals, adapt the game above. Provide each child with a '0·1–1·2 number card'. Say: *Everyone stand up. …Sit down if the number on your card is the answer to 0·7 divided by 7. (0·1)*

For the 8 multiplication table

To recall the multiplication facts for the 8 multiplication table:

- Provide each child with a 'Multiples of 8 number card'.
- Say: *Everyone stand up. Look at the number on your card. Sit down if the number on your card is the answer to:*
  - *1 times 8 (8)*
  - *6 times 8 (48)*
  - *11 multiplied by 8 (88)*
  - *9 times 8 (72)*
  - *8 multiplied by 8 (64)*
  - *the product of 4 and 8 (32)*
  - *2 multiplied by 8 (16)*
  - *7 times 8 (56)*
  - *the product of 5 and 8 (40)*
  - *12 multiplied by 8 (96)*
  - *the product of 10 and 8 (80)*

The winners are the children still standing with 24 on their cards.

To use the multiplication facts for the 8 multiplication table to recall related facts involving multiples of 10, adapt the game above. Provide each child with a 'Multiples of 80 number card'. Say: *Everyone stand up…Sit down if the number on your card is the answer to 1 times 80. (80)*

To use the multiplication facts for the 8 multiplication table to recall related facts involving decimals, adapt the game above. Provide each child with a 'Multiples of 0·8 number card'. Say: *Everyone stand up…Sit down if the number on your card is the answer to 1 times 0·8. (0·8)*

Who's left standing?

(continued)

To recall the division facts for the 8 multiplication table:

- Provide each child with a '1–12 number card'.
- Say: *Everyone stand up. Look at the number on your card. Sit down if the number on your card is the answer to:*
  - *64 divided by 8* (8)
  - *8 divided into 72* (9)
  - *96 divided by 8* (12)
  - *8 divided into 24* (3)
  - *88 divided by 8* (11)
  - *8 divided into 40* (5)
  - *80 divided by 8* (10)
  - *48 divided by 8* (6)
  - *8 divided into 16* (2)
  - *56 divided by 8* (7)
  - *8 divided by 8* (1)

The winners are the children still standing with 4 on their cards.

To use the division facts for the 8 multiplication table to recall related facts involving multiples of 80, adapt the game above. Provide each child with a 'Multiples of 10 number card'. Say: *Everyone stand up…Sit down if the number on your card is the answer to 640 divided by 8.* (80)

To use the division facts for the 8 multiplication table to recall related facts involving decimals, adapt the game above. Provide each child with a '0·1–1·2 number card'. Say: *Everyone stand up…Sit down if the number on your card is the answer to 6·4 divided by 8.* (0·8)

For the 9 multiplication table

To recall the multiplication facts for the 9 multiplication table:

- Provide each child with a 'Multiples of 9 number card'.
- Say: *Everyone stand up. Look at the number on your card. Sit down if the number on your card is the answer to:*
  - *3 times 9* (27)
  - *8 multiplied by 9* (72)
  - *4 times 9* (36)
  - *the product of 6 and 9* (54)
  - *1 times 9* (9)
  - *the product of 12 and 9* (108)
  - *7 multiplied by 9* (63)
  - *2 times 9* (18)
  - *the product of 9 and 5* (45)
  - *10 multiplied by 9* (90)
  - *11 times 9* (99)

The winners are the children still standing with 81 on their cards.

To use the multiplication facts for the 9 multiplication table to recall related facts involving multiples of 10, adapt the game above. Provide each child with a 'Multiples of 90 number card'. Say: *Everyone stand up…Sit down if the number on your card is the answer to 3 times 90.* (270)

To use the multiplication facts for the 9 multiplication table to recall related facts involving decimals, adapt the game above. Provide each child with a 'Multiples of 0·9 number card'. Say: *Everyone stand up…Sit down if the number on your card is the answer to 3 times 0·9.* (2·7)

(continued)

Who's left standing?

(continued)

To recall the division facts for the 9 multiplication table:

- Provide each child with a '1–12 number card'.
- Say: *Everyone stand up. Look at the number on your card. Sit down if the number on your card is the answer to:*
  - *54 divided by 9* (6)
  - *108 divided by 9* (12)
  - *9 divided into 18* (2)
  - *9 divided into 27* (3)
  - *63 divided by 9* (7)
  - *90 divided by 9* (10)
  - *9 divided into 45* (5)
  - *9 divided into 81* (9)
  - *9 divided by 9* (1)
  - *99 divided by 9* (11)
  - *36 divided by 9* (4)

The winners are the children still standing with 8 on their cards.

To use the division facts for the 9 multiplication table to recall related facts involving multiples of 90, adapt the game above. Provide each child with a 'Multiples of 10 number card'. Say: *Everyone stand up…Sit down if the number on your card is the answer to 540 divided by 9.* (60)

To use the division facts for the 9 multiplication table to recall related facts involving decimals, adapt the game above. Provide each child with a '0·1–1·2 number card'. Say: *Everyone stand up…Sit down if the number on your card is the answer to 5·4 divided by 9.* (0·6)

For the 10 multiplication table

To recall the multiplication facts for the 10 multiplication table:

- Provide each child with a 'Multiples of 10 number card'.
- Say: *Everyone stand up. Look at the number on your card. Sit down if the number on your card is the answer to:*
  - *9 multiplied by 10* (90)
  - *11 multiplied by 10* (110)
  - *the product of 5 and 10* (50)
  - *7 times 10* (70)
  - *10 multiplied by 10* (100)
  - *2 times 10* (20)
  - *the product of 8 and 10* (80)
  - *12 times 10* (120)
  - *6 times 10* (60)
  - *1 multiplied by 10* (10)
  - *4 times 10* (40)

The winners are the children still standing with 30 on their cards.

To use the multiplication facts for the 10 multiplication table to recall related facts involving multiples of 10, adapt the game above. Provide each child with a 'Multiples of 100 number card'. Say: *Everyone stand up…Sit down if the number on your card is the answer to 9 multiplied by 100.* (900)

Who's left standing?

(continued)

To recall the division facts for the 10 multiplication table:

- Provide each child with a '1–12 number card'.
- Say: *Everyone stand up. Look at the number on your card. Sit down if the number on your card is the answer to:*
    - *80 divided by 10 (8)*
    - *10 divided into 20 (2)*
    - *100 divided by 10 (10)*
    - *120 divided by 10 (12)*
    - *110 divided by 10 (11)*
    - *70 divided by 10 (7)*
    - *40 divided by 10 (4)*
    - *10 divided into 90 (9)*
    - *10 divided by 10 (1)*
    - *10 divided into 30 (3)*
    - *10 divided into 50 (5)*

The winners are the children still standing with 6 on their cards.

To use the division facts for the 10 multiplication table to recall related facts involving multiples of 100, adapt the game above. Provide each child with a 'Multiples of 10 number card'. Say: *Everyone stand up…Sit down if the number on your card is the answer to 800 divided by 10. (80)*

To use the division facts for the 10 multiplication table to recall related facts involving decimals, adapt the game above. Provide each child with a '0·1–1·2 number card'. Say: *Everyone stand up…Sit down if the number on your card is the answer to 8 divided by 10. (0·8)*

For the 11 multiplication table

To recall the multiplication facts for the 11 multiplication table:

- Provide each child with a 'Multiples of 11 number card'.
- Say: *Everyone stand up. Look at the number on your card. Sit down if the number on your card is the answer to:*
    - *6 times 11 (66)*
    - *2 times 11 (22)*
    - *9 multiplied by 11 (99)*
    - *8 times 11 (88)*
    - *1 times 11 (11)*
    - *the product of 3 and 11 (33)*
    - *12 multiplied by 11 (132)*
    - *7 times 11 (77)*
    - *the product of 10 and 11 (110)*
    - *11 multiplied by 11 (121)*
    - *the product of 4 and 11 (44)*

The winners are the children still standing with 55 on their cards.

To use the multiplication facts for the 11 multiplication table to recall related facts involving multiples of 10, adapt the game above. Provide each child with a 'Multiples of 110 number card'. Say: *Everyone stand up…Sit down if the number on your card is the answer to 6 times 110. (660)*

To use the multiplication facts for the 11 multiplication table to recall related facts involving decimals, adapt the game above. Provide each child with a 'Multiples of 1·1 number card'. Say: *Everyone stand up…Sit down if the number on your card is the answer to 6 times 1·1. (6·6)*

(continued)

Who's left standing?

(continued)

To recall the division facts for the 11 multiplication table:

- Provide each child with a '1–12 number card'.
- Say: *Everyone stand up. Look at the number on your card. Sit down if the number on your card is the answer to:*

  - *110 divided by 11 (10)*
  - *44 divided by 11 (4)*
  - *11 divided into 99 (9)*
  - *66 divided by 11 (6)*

  - *77 divided by 11 (7)*
  - *11 divided by 11 (1)*
  - *11 divided into 33 (3)*
  - *121 divided by 11 (11)*

  - *11 divided into 132 (12)*
  - *88 divided by 11 (8)*
  - *11 divided into 22 (2)*

The winners are the children still standing with 5 on their cards.

To use the division facts for the 11 multiplication table to recall related facts involving multiples of 110, adapt the game above. Provide each child with a 'Multiples of 10 number card'. Say: *Everyone stand up…Sit down if the number on your card is the answer to 1100 divided by 11. (100)*

To use the division facts for the 11 multiplication table to recall related facts involving decimals, adapt the game above. Provide each child with a '0·1–1·2 number card'. Say: *Everyone stand up…Sit down if the number on your card is the answer to 11 divided by 11. (1)*

For the 12 multiplication table

To recall the multiplication facts for the 12 multiplication table:

- Provide each child with a 'Multiples of 12 number card'.
- Say: *Everyone stand up. Look at the number on your card. Sit down if the number on your card is the answer to:*

  - *5 times 12 (60)*
  - *4 times 12 (48)*
  - *11 multiplied by 12 (132)*
  - *1 times 12 (12)*

  - *12 multiplied by 12 (144)*
  - *the product of 6 and 12 (72)*
  - *2 multiplied by 12 (24)*
  - *10 times 12 (120)*

  - *the product of 3 and 12 (36)*
  - *9 multiplied by 12 (108)*
  - *the product of 12 and 8 (96)*

The winners are the children still standing with 84 on their cards.

To use the multiplication facts for the 12 multiplication table to recall related facts involving multiples of 10, adapt the game above. Provide each child with a 'Multiples of 120 number card'. Say: *Everyone stand up…Sit down if the number on your card is the answer to 5 times 120. (600)*

To use the multiplication facts for the 12 multiplication table to recall related facts involving decimals adapt the game above. Provide each child with a 'Multiples of 1·2 number card'. Say: *Everyone stand up…Sit down if the number on your card is the answer to 5 times 1·2. (6)*

Who's left standing?

(continued)

To recall the division facts for the 12 multiplication table:

* Provide each child with a '1–12 number card'.

* Say: *Everyone stand up. Look at the number on your card. Sit down if the number on your card is the answer to:*

– *12 divided into 36* (3)	– *96 divided by 12* (8)	– *132 divided by 12* (11)
– *12 divided into 60* (5)	– *84 divided by 12* (7)	– *12 divided by 12* (1)
– *48 divided by 12* (4)	– *12 divided into 24* (2)	– *120 divided by 12* (10)
– *144 divided by 12* (12)	– *12 divided into 72* (6)	

The winners are the children still standing with 9 on their cards.

To use the division facts for the 12 multiplication table to recall related facts involving multiples of 120, adapt the game above. Provide each child with a 'Multiples of 10 number card'. Say: *Everyone stand up…Sit down if the number on your card is the answer to 12 divided into 360.* (30)

To use the division facts for the 12 multiplication table to recall related facts involving decimals, adapt the game above. Provide each child with a '0·1–1·2 number card'. Say: *Everyone stand up…Sit down if the number on your card is the answer to 12 divided into 3·6.* (0·3)

Forming groups

Objectives

- Recall and use multiplication and division facts for multiplication tables up to 12 × 12
- Multiply and divide numbers mentally drawing upon known facts

Teacher resources

- none

Pupil resources

- '2-digit number cards' or 'Multiples of…number cards' (one card per child)

What to do

- Decide which multiplication table you want the children to practise and consolidate and provide each child with either one of the corresponding 'Multiples of…number cards' or one of the '2-digit number cards'. (**Note:** It is recommended that you use the 'Multiples of…number cards' and '2-digit number cards' provided on the CD-ROM.)

- If, for example, you are practising the 9 times table, point and say: *Everyone stand up. Look at the number on your card. When I say 'Go!' I want everyone who has a card with a number on it that is a multiple of 9 to move to this side of the room, and everyone who has a card with a number on it that is not a multiple of 9 to move to this side of the room. Ready? Go!*

- Once the two groups have formed, ask the members of each group in turn to call out their number. Say: *Everyone hold up your number card. The multiples of 9 group, starting with Lisa call out your numbers. Now the group that have cards that are not multiples of 9, starting with Rav, tell us your numbers.*

- If appropriate, ask each group to order themselves smallest to largest.

Variations

- Rather than providing each child with a 'Multiples of…number card' or a '2-digit number card', use two different sets of multiples cards to provide each child with a card, for example, the 'Multiples of 9 number cards' and the 'Multiples of 6 number cards'. Do the children that have the cards that are common multiples, for example, 54, realise that they belong to both groups?
- Use the 'Multiples of 20 / 30 / 40 / 50 / 60 / 70 / 80 / 90 / 100 / 110 / 120 number cards'.
- Use the 'Multiples of 0·2 / 0·3 / 0·4 / 0·5 / 0·6 / 0·7 / 0·8 / 0·9 / (1–12 number cards) / 1·1 / 1·2 number cards'.

Stand up

Objectives

- Recall and use multiplication and division facts for multiplication tables up to 12 × 12
- Multiply and divide numbers mentally drawing upon known facts

Teacher resources

- none

Pupil resources

Number cards

- '1–12 number cards' (one card per child)

What to do

- Decide which multiplication or division facts for the multiplication tables up to 12 × 12 you want the children to practise and consolidate.
- Provide each child with a '1–12 number card'.

For the 2 multiplication table

To recall the multiplication facts for the 2 multiplication table:

- Say: *Look at the number on your card. Multiply the number on your card by 2. Stand up if the answer is 14.*
- Ask: *Who can tell me what number is on Tina's and Sanjay's cards?* (7)
- Ask the children standing to show their cards.
- The children standing then sit down.
- Repeat saying: *Multiply the number on your card by 2. Stand up if the answer is:*

4 (2)	16 (8)	8 (4)	6 (3)	10 (5)	2 (1)
22 (11)	20 (10)	12 (6)	18 (9)	24 (12)	

To use the multiplication facts for the 2 multiplication table to recall related facts involving multiples of 10:

- Say: *Look at the number on your card. Multiply the number on your card by 20. Stand up if the answer is:*

140 (7)	160 (8)	80 (4)	60 (3)	100 (5)	20 (1)
220 (11)	200 (10)	120 (6)	180 (9)	240 (12)	40 (2)

To use the multiplication facts for the 2 multiplication table to recall related facts involving decimals:

- Say: *Look at the number on your card. Multiply the number on your card by 0·2. Stand up if the answer is:*

1·4 (7)	1·6 (8)	0·8 (4)	0·6 (3)	1 (5)	0·2 (1)
2·2 (11)	2 (10)	1·2 (6)	1·8 (9)	2·4 (12)	0·4 (2)

(continued)

Stand up

(continued)

To recall the division facts for the 2 multiplication table:

- Say: *Divide 24 by 2. Look at the number on your card. If you have the answer on your card, stand up.*
- Ask: *Who can tell me what number is on Michael's and Sarah's cards?* (12)
- Ask the children standing to show their cards.
- The children standing then sit down.
- Repeat for the following:

2 (1)	22 (11)	8 (4)	14 (7)	18 (9)	12 (6)
6 (3)	16 (8)	10 (5)	20 (10)	4 (2)	

To use the division facts for the 2 multiplication table to recall related facts involving multiples of 10:

- Say: *Divide 240 by 20. Look at the number on your card. If you have the answer on your card, stand up.* (12) Repeat for the following:

120 (6)	220 (11)	80 (4)	140 (7)	180 (9)	20 (1)
60 (3)	160 (8)	100 (5)	200 (10)	40 (2)	

Variations

For the 3 multiplication table

To recall the multiplication facts for the 3 multiplication table:

- Say: *Look at the number on your card. Multiply the number on your card by 3. Stand up if the answer is:*

27 (9)	12 (4)	3 (1)	18 (6)	30 (10)	33 (11)
6 (2)	21 (7)	24 (8)	9 (3)	36 (12)	15 (5)

To use the multiplication facts for the 3 multiplication table to recall related facts involving multiples of 10, adapt the game above. For example, say: *Multiply the number on your card by 30. Stand up if the answer is 270.* (9)

To use the multiplication facts for the 3 multiplication table to recall related facts involving decimals, adapt the game above. For example, say: *Multiply the number on your card by 0·3. Stand up if the answer is 2·7.* (9)

To recall the division facts for the 3 multiplication table:

- Say: *Divide 21 by 3. Look at the number on your card. If you have the answer on your card, stand up.* (7) Repeat for the following:

30 (10)	27 (9)	9 (3)	15 (5)	33 (11)	12 (4)
24 (8)	3 (1)	6 (2)	36 (12)	18 (6)	

To use the division facts for the 3 multiplication table to recall related facts involving multiples of 10, adapt the game above. For example, say: *Divide 210 by 30. Look at the number on your card. If you have the answer on your card, stand up.* (7)

Stand up

(continued)

For the 4 multiplication table

To recall the multiplication facts for the 4 multiplication table:

- Say: *Look at the number on your card. Multiply the number on your card by 4. Stand up if the answer is:*

48 (12)	12 (3)	20 (5)	8 (2)	40 (10)	24 (6)
16 (4)	28 (7)	32 (8)	36 (9)	4 (1)	44 (11)

To use the multiplication facts for the 4 multiplication table to recall related facts involving multiples of 10, adapt the game above. For example, say: *Multiply the number on your card by 40. Stand up if the answer is 480.* (12)

To use the multiplication facts for the 4 multiplication table to recall related facts involving decimals, adapt the game above. For example, say: *Multiply the number on your card by 0·4. Stand up if the answer is 4·8.* (12)

To recall the division facts for the 4 multiplication table:

- Say: *Divide 36 by 4. Look at the number on your card. If you have the answer on your card, stand up.* (9) Repeat for the following:

44 (11)	48 (12)	24 (6)	8 (2)	32 (8)	12 (3)
4 (1)	16 (4)	40 (10)	20 (5)	28 (7)	

To use the division facts for the 4 multiplication table to recall related facts involving multiples of 10, adapt the game above. For example, say: *Divide 360 by 40. Look at the number on your card. If you have the answer on your card, stand up.* (9)

For the 5 multiplication table

To recall the multiplication facts for the 5 multiplication table:

- Say: *Look at the number on your card. Multiply the number on your card by 5. Stand up if the answer is:*

55 (11)	5 (1)	25 (5)	30 (6)	10 (2)	45 (9)
40 (8)	50 (10)	35 (7)	20 (4)	60 (12)	15 (3)

To use the multiplication facts for the 5 multiplication table to recall related facts involving multiples of 10, adapt the game above. For example, say: *Multiply the number on your card by 50. Stand up if the answer is 550.* (11)

To use the multiplication facts for the 5 multiplication table to recall related facts involving decimals, adapt the game above. For example, say: *Multiply the number on your card by 0·5. Stand up if the answer is 5·5. (11)*

(continued)

Stand up

(continued)

To recall the division facts for the 5 multiplication table:

- Say: *Divide 25 by 5. Look at the number on your card. If you have the answer on your card, stand up.* (5). Repeat for the following:

35 (7)	5 (1)	55 (11)	30 (6)	20 (4)	10 (2)
40 (8)	60 (12)	45 (9)	15 (3)	50 (10)	

To use the division facts for the 5 multiplication table to recall related facts involving multiples of 10 adapt the game above, for example, Say: *Divide 250 by 50. Look at the number on your card. If you have the answer on your card, stand up.* (5)

For the 6 multiplication table

To recall the multiplication facts for the 6 multiplication table:

- Say: *Look at the number on your card. Multiply the number on your card by 6. Stand up if the answer is:*

18 (3)	30 (5)	54 (9)	48 (8)	12 (2)	36 (6)
24 (4)	6 (1)	42 (7)	66 (11)	72 (12)	60 (10)

To use the multiplication facts for the 6 multiplication table to recall related facts involving multiples of 10, adapt the game above. For example, say: *Multiply the number on your card by 60. Stand up if the answer is 180.* (3)

To use the multiplication facts for the 6 multiplication table to recall related facts involving decimals, adapt the game above. For example, say: *Multiply the number on your card by 0·6. Stand up if the answer is 1·8.* (3)

To recall the division facts for the 6 multiplication table:

- Say: *Divide 54 by 6. Look at the number on your card. If you have the answer on your card, stand up.* (9) Repeat for the following:

48 (8)	6 (1)	60 (10)	12 (2)	42 (7)	24 (4)
18 (3)	36 (6)	66 (11)	72 (12)	30 (5)	

To use the division facts for the 6 multiplication table to recall related facts involving multiples of 10, adapt the game above. For example, say: *Divide 540 by 60. Look at the number on your card. If you have the answer on your card, stand up.* (9)

For the 7 multiplication table

To recall the multiplication facts for the 7 multiplication table:

- Say: *Look at the number on your card. Multiply the number on your card by 7. Stand up if the answer is:*

56 (8)	63 (9)	35 (5)	77 (11)	28 (4)	49 (7)
84 (12)	7 (1)	14 (2)	70 (10)	42 (6)	21 (3)

Stand up

(continued)

To use the multiplication facts for the 7 multiplication table to recall related facts involving multiples of 10 adapt the game above. For example, say: *Multiply the number on your card by 70. Stand up if the answer is 560.* (8)

To use the multiplication facts for the 7 multiplication table to recall related facts involving decimals adapt the game above. For example, say: *Multiply the number on your card by 0·7. Stand up if the answer is 5·6.* (8)

To recall the division facts for the 7 multiplication table:

* Say: *Divide 42 by 7. Look at the number on your card. If you have the answer on your card, stand up.* (6) Repeat for the following:

84 (12)	35 (5)	28 (4)	49 (7)	70 (10)	14 (2)
21 (3)	56 (8)	7 (1)	63 (9)	77 (11)	

To use the division facts for the 7 multiplication table to recall related facts involving multiples of 10, adapt the game above. For example, say: *Divide 420 by 70. Look at the number on your card. If you have the answer on your card, stand up.* (6)

For the 8 multiplication table

To recall the multiplication facts for the 8 multiplication table:

* Say: *Look at the number on your card. Multiply the number on your card by 8. Stand up if the answer is:*

64 (8)	24 (3)	80 (10)	56 (7)	32 (4)	40 (5)
16 (2)	72 (9)	8 (1)	88 (11)	48 (6)	96 (12)

To use the multiplication facts for the 8 multiplication table to recall related facts involving multiples of 10, adapt the game above. For example, say: *Multiply the number on your card by 80. Stand up if the answer is 640.* (8)

To use the multiplication facts for the 8 multiplication table to recall related facts involving decimals, adapt the game above. For example, say: *Multiply the number on your card by 0·8. Stand up if the answer is 6·4.* (8)

To recall the division facts for the 8 multiplication table:

* Say: *Divide 32 by 8. Look at the number on your card. If you have the answer on your card, stand up.* (4) Repeat for the following:

48 (6)	40 (5)	80 (10)	8 (1)	24 (3)	72 (9)
56 (7)	96 (12)	88 (11)	16 (2)	64 (8)	

To use the division facts for the 8 multiplication table to recall related facts involving multiples of 10, adapt the game above. For example, say: *Divide 320 by 80. Look at the number on your card. If you have the answer on your card, stand up.* (4)

(continued)

Stand up

(continued)

For the 9 multiplication table

To recall the multiplication facts for the 9 multiplication table:

- Say: *Look at the number on your card. Multiply the number on your card by 9. Stand up if the answer is:*

54 (6)	90 (10)	72 (8)	45 (5)	99 (11)	36 (4)
108 (12)	27 (3)	9 (1)	18 (2)	81 (9)	63 (7)

To use the multiplication facts for the 9 multiplication table to recall related facts involving multiples of 10, adapt the game above. For example, say: *Multiply the number on your card by 90. Stand up if the answer is 540.* (6)

To use the multiplication facts for the 9 multiplication table to recall related facts involving decimals, adapt the game above. For example, say: *Multiply the number on your card by 0·9. Stand up if the answer is 5·4.* (6)

To recall the division facts for the 9 multiplication table:

- Say: *Divide 63 by 9. Look at the number on your card. If you have the answer on your card, stand up.* (7) Repeat for the following:

45 (5)	72 (8)	108 (12)	36 (4)	81 (9)	27 (3)
9 (1)	54 (6)	90 (10)	99 (11)	18 (2)	

To use the division facts for the 9 multiplication table to recall related facts involving multiples of 10, adapt the game above. For example, say: *Divide 630 by 90. Look at the number on your card. If you have the answer on your card, stand up.* (7)

For the 10 multiplication table

To recall the multiplication facts for the 10 multiplication table:

- Say: *Look at the number on your card. Multiply the number on your card by 10. Stand up if the answer is:*

40 (4)	100 (10)	70 (7)	30 (3)	90 (9)	80 (8)
110 (11)	20 (2)	50 (5)	120 (12)	10 (1)	60 (6)

To use the multiplication facts for the 10 multiplication table to recall related facts involving multiples of 10, adapt the game above. For example, say: *Multiply the number on your card by 100. Stand up if the answer is 400.* (4)

To recall the division facts for the 10 multiplication table:

- Say: *Divide 20 by 10. Look at the number on your card. If you have the answer on your card, stand up.* (2) Repeat for the following:

90 (9)	70 (7)	100 (10)	60 (6)	50 (5)	110 (11)
120 (12)	30 (3)	10 (1)	40 (4)	80 (8)	

Stand up

(continued)

To use the division facts for the 10 multiplication table to recall related facts involving multiples of 10, adapt the game above. For example, say: *Divide 200 by 100. Look at the number on your card. If you have the answer on your card, stand up.* (2)

For the 11 multiplication table

To recall the multiplication facts for the 11 multiplication table:

* Say: *Look at the number on your card. Multiply the number on your card by 11. Stand up if the answer is:*

88 (8)	132 (12)	66 (6)	44 (4)	99 (9)	22 (2)
11 (1)	55 (5)	110 (10)	33 (3)	121 (11)	77 (7)

To use the multiplication facts for the 11 multiplication table to recall related facts involving multiples of 10, adapt the game above. For example, say: *Multiply the number on your card by 110. Stand up if the answer is 880.* (8)

To use the multiplication facts for the 11 multiplication table to recall related facts involving decimals, adapt the game above. For example, say: *Multiply the number on your card by 1·1. Stand up if the answer is 8·8.* (8)

To recall the division facts for the 11 multiplication table:

* Say: *Divide 55 by 11. Look at the number on your card. If you have the answer on your card, stand up.* (5) Repeat for the following:

99 (9)	33 (3)	88 (8)	132 (12)	11 (1)	22 (2)
77 (7)	44 (4)	121 (11)	66 (6)	110 (10)	

To use the division facts for the 11 multiplication table to recall related facts involving multiples of 10, adapt the game above. For example, say: *Divide 550 by 110. Look at the number on your card. If you have the answer on your card, stand up.* (5)

For the 12 multiplication table

To recall the multiplication facts for the 12 multiplication table:

* Say: *Look at the number on your card. Multiply the number on your card by 12. Stand up if the answer is:*

72 (6)	36 (3)	132 (11)	108 (9)	60 (5)	48 (4)
24 (2)	144 (12)	120 (10)	96 (8)	12 (1)	84 (7)

(continued)

Stand up

(continued)

To use the multiplication facts for the 12 multiplication table to recall related facts involving multiples of 10, adapt the game above. For example, say: *Multiply the number on your card by 120. Stand up if the answer is 720.* (6)

To use the multiplication facts for the 12 multiplication table to recall related facts involving decimals, adapt the game above. For example, say: *Multiply the number on your card by 1·2. Stand up if the answer is 7·2.* (6)

To practise the division facts for the 12 multiplication table:

* Say: *Divide 36 by 12. Look at the number on your card. If you have the answer on your card, stand up.* (3) Repeat for the following:

72 (6)	96 (8)	48 (4)	84 (7)	24 (2)
132 (11)	120 (10)	60 (5)	12 (1)	108 (9)	144 (12)

To use the division facts for the 12 multiplication table to recall related facts involving multiples of 10, adapt the game above. For example, say: *Divide 360 by 120. Look at the number on your card. If you have the answer on your card, stand up.* (3)

Whole-class, paired or individual activities

Using the Maths Facts in the *Facts and Games* book

Objectives

- Recall and use multiplication and division facts for multiplication tables up to 12 × 12
- Multiply and divide numbers mentally drawing upon known facts

Teacher resources

Maths Facts   Multiplication and division

Pupil resources

- *Fluency in Number Facts: Facts and Games: Years 5 & 6* book pages 19–43 (per child or pair)

Introduction

The Maths Facts on pages 19–43 of the *Fluency in Number Facts: Facts and Games: Years 5 & 6* book cover the key multiplication and division number facts that children should be able to recall instantly by the end of Upper Key Stage 2.

These pages aim to develop children's fluency by:

- securing a thorough conceptual understanding of the multiplication and division number facts
- identifying patterns and the relationship between multiplication and division
- developing strategic approaches to recalling and deriving the answers to multiplication and division number facts.

To assist in achieving these aims, the multiplication and division number facts contained in the *Facts and Games: Years 5 & 6* book are presented in the following ways:

- Multiplication tables to 12 × 12 and involving multiples of 10 (pages 19–22)
- Division facts relating to the multiplication tables to 12 × 12 and involving multiples of 10 (pages 23–26)
- Multiples up to 12 × 12 (pages 27 and 28)
- Multiplication square to 12 × 12 (pages 29 and 30)
- Multiples of 10 multiplication square (page 31)
- Decimals multiplication square (page 32)
- Trios for the multiplication facts to 12 × 12 (pages 33–43)

The following pages include a brief description of each of these presentations, along with suggestions of how to focus on these Maths Facts either with the whole class, or with children working in pairs or individually.

(continued)

Whole-class, paired or individual activities

Using the Maths Facts in the *Facts and Games book*

(continued)

Multiplication tables to 12 × 12 and involving multiples of 10 (pages 19–22)

These pages show the times tables facts for the multiplication tables to 12 × 12 and the related facts involving multiples of 10.

The 2, 4 and 8 times tables are in red, the 3, 6 and 12 times tables in green, and the 5 and 10 times tables in blue. This corresponds with the colours used on pages 23–43. The use of colour has been used to highlight the relationship between different multiplication tables.

These pages also show the four 'keys facts', i.e. 1 ×, 2 ×, 5 × and 10 ×, for each of the multiplication tables to 12 × 12. These 'key facts', once secure, should be used to derive related facts involving multiples of 10 and 100, as well as those involving decimals.

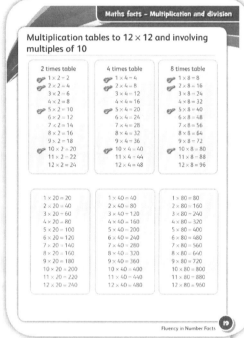

How to use the Maths Facts

 Whole class

- Display the appropriate PDF file (CD-ROM / Maths Facts / Multiplication and division) and provide each child or pair with a copy of the *Facts and Games: Years 5 & 6* book and direct their attention to the relevant multiplication facts on pages 19–22.

- Begin by asking the children to identify different patterns and relationships in the list of calculations and discuss these with the class.

- Draw children's attention to the four 'key facts', i.e. 1 ×, 2 ×, 5 × and 10 × and remind them how these 'key facts' can help them derive answers to unknown related facts. For example:

- Also draw children's attention to the use of colour: i.e. the 2, 4 and 8 times tables are in red, the 3, 6 and 12 times tables in green, and the 5 and 10 times tables in blue. Remind children of the relationships between different multiplication tables:

  - the answers to the 4 times table are double the answers to the 2 times table, for example, 3 × 2 = 6 and 3 × 4 = 12

  - the answers to the 8 times table are double the answers to the 4 times table, for example, 3 × 4 = 12 and 3 × 8 = 24

  - the answers to the 6 times table are double the answers to the 3 times table, for example, 7 × 3 = 21 and 7 × 6 = 42

  - the answers to the 12 times table are double the answers to the 6 times table, for example, 7 × 6 = 42 and 7 × 12 = 84.

- Ensure the children realise that, just like the 'key facts', knowing the relationship between different multiplication tables can help them derive the answers to unknown facts.

Whole-class, paired or individual activities

Using the Maths Facts in the *Facts and Games* book

(continued)

- Also discuss with the children how knowing the multiplication facts for the multiplication tables up to 12 × 12, and using and applying the commutative law, can help them derive answers to related number facts involving:
  - multiples of 10 and 100, for example, 6 × 12 = 72, therefore 60 × 12 = 720, 6 × 120 = 720; 600 × 12 = 7200 and 60 × 120 = 7200
  - decimals, for example, 6 × 12 = 72, therefore 0·6 × 12 = 7·2 and 6 × 1·2 = 7·2.
- Repeat for other multiplication facts and the related facts involving multiples of 10 and 100, as well as those involving decimals.
- Conclude by hiding the PDF file, asking the children to close their copy of the *Facts and Games: Years 5 & 6* book and ask them questions similar to the following:
  - *What is 7 times 12?*
  - *What is 9 multiplied by 12?*
  - *What is the product of 8 and 12?*
  - *12 and what other number when multiplied together make 60?*
  - *If you know that 8 times 12 is 96, what is the answer to 80 times 12? What about 8 times 120? What about 0·8 multiplied by 12?*

Pairs

- Provide each pair with a copy of the *Facts and Games: Years 5 & 6* book and direct their attention to the relevant multiplication facts on pages 19–22. Alternatively, ask the children to choose a multiplication table that they know they need to develop greater fluency of.
- Children spend just two or three minutes individually looking at the multiplication facts with the aim of developing greater fluency of the facts.
- Children then take turns to take charge of the book and ask each other questions similar to those above, including those involving multiples of 10 and 100, as well as those involving decimals.

Individual

- Provide the child with a copy of the *Facts and Games: Years 5 & 6* book and direct their attention to the relevant multiplication facts on pages 19–22. Alternatively, ask the child to choose a multiplication table that they know they need to develop greater fluency of.
- It is recommended that the child spend just five or ten minutes each time, focussing their attention on developing greater fluency of the facts.
- To provide some personal challenge, suggest the child:
  - covers the multiplication facts and recites the facts to themselves
  - recalls the related facts involving multiples of 10 and 100, as well as those involving decimals.

(continued)

Whole-class, paired or individual activities

Using the Maths Facts in the *Facts and Games* book

(continued)

Division facts relating to the multiplication tables to 12 × 12 and involving multiples of 10 (pages 23–26)

These pages show the division facts for the multiplication tables to 12 × 12 and the related facts involving multiples of 10.

The division facts for the 2, 4 and 8 multiplication tables are in red, the division facts for the 3, 6 and 12 multiplication tables in green, and the division facts for the 5 and 10 multiplication tables in blue. This corresponds with the colours used on pages 19–22 and 27–43. The use of colour has been used to highlight the relationship between different multiplication tables.

At this stage children should be able to use these division facts and apply their knowledge of the relationship between multiplication and division to derive related facts involving multiples of 10 and 100, as well as those involving decimals.

How to use the Maths Facts

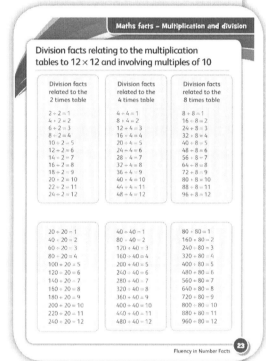

 Whole class

- Display the appropriate PDF file (CD-ROM / Maths Facts / Multiplication and division) and provide each child or pair with a copy of the *Facts and Games: Years 5 & 6* book and direct their attention to the relevant division facts on pages 23–26.

- Begin by asking the children to identify different patterns and relationships in the list of calculations and discuss these with the class.

- Draw children's attention to the corresponding multiplication facts on the appropriate PDF file and pages 19–22 of the *Facts and Games: Years 5 & 6* book. In particular, ensure they are made aware of how the same colour has been used to link the related multiplication and division facts.

- Remind the children of the inverse relationship between multiplication and division and how they can use a known multiplication fact to help them derive the answer to an unknown division fact (and vice versa), for example, 8 × 12 = 96 and 96 ÷ 12 = 8.

- Next, discuss with the children how knowing the division facts for the multiplication tables up to 12 × 12 can help them derive answers to related number facts involving:
  - multiples of 10 and 100, for example, 96 ÷ 12 = 8, therefore 960 ÷ 12 = 80, 9600 ÷ 12 = 800 and 960 ÷ 120 = 8
  - decimals, for example, 96 ÷ 12 = 8, therefore 9·6 ÷ 12 = 0·8 and if appropriate, 9·6 ÷ 1·2 = 8.

Whole-class, paired or individual activities

Using the Maths Facts in the *Facts and Games* book

(continued)

- Repeat for other division facts and the related facts involving multiples of 10 and 100, as well as those involving decimals.

- Conclude by hiding the PDF file, asking the children to close their copy of the *Facts and Games: Years 5 & 6* book and ask them questions similar to the following:

  - *What is 72 divided by 12?*
  - *What is 12 divided into 132?*
  - *How many twelves are there in 36?*
  - *If you know that 96 divided by 12 is 8, what is the answer to 960 divided by 12? What about 9600 divided by 12? What about 9·6 divided by 12?*

Pairs

- Provide each pair with a copy of the *Facts and Games: Years 5 & 6* book and direct their attention to the relevant division facts on pages 23–26. Alternatively, ask the children to choose the division facts that they know they need to develop greater fluency of.

- Children spend just two or three minutes individually looking at the division facts with the aim of developing greater fluency of the facts.

- Children then take turns to take charge of the book and ask each other questions similar to those above, including those involving multiples of 10 and 100, as well as those involving decimals.

Individual

- Provide the child with a copy of the *Facts and Games: Years 5 & 6* book and direct their attention to the relevant division facts on pages 23–26. Alternatively, ask the children to choose the division facts that they know they need to develop greater fluency of.

- It is recommended that the child spends just five or ten minutes each time, focussing their attention on developing greater fluency of the facts.

- To provide some personal challenge, suggest the child:
  - covers the division facts and recites the facts to themselves
  - recalls the related facts involving multiples of 10 and 100, as well as those involving decimals.

(continued)

Whole-class, paired or individual activities

Using the Maths Facts in the *Facts and Games* book

(continued)

Multiples up to 12 × 12 (pages 27 and 28)

These pages show the multiplication and related division facts for 2, 3, 4, 5, 6, 7, 8, 9, 10, 11 and 12 up to the 12th multiple, for example, 24 (× 2), 48 (× 4) and 96 (× 8).

The multiples of 2, 4 and 8 are in red, the multiples of 3, 6 and 12 in green, and the multiples of 5 and 10 in blue. This corresponds with the colours used on pages 19–26 and 29–41. The use of colour has been used to highlight the relationship between different multiplication tables.

These number lines are a simple way of showing the relationship between the increasing steps and the corresponding products. They also highlight the link between multiplication and division.

How to use the Maths Facts

  Whole class

- Display the appropriate PDF file (CD-ROM / Maths Facts / Multiplication and division) and provide each child or pair with a copy of the *Facts and Games: Years 5 & 6* book and direct their attention to the relevant number line on pages 27 and 28.

- Remind the children how the line is simply a number line, but instead of having one set of numbers along the line, there are two sets of numbers – one set above the line (the numbers 1 to 12) and another set below the line (the corresponding multiples).

- Ask the children to identify any patterns and relationships between the numbers on the number line.

- Then, pointing in turn to each of the numbers 1 to 12 above the number line, and then the corresponding multiples below the line, say the multiplication facts to the children, for example:
  - *1 times 12 is 12*
  - *2 times 12 is 24*
  - *3 times 12 is 36*
  - *4 times 12 is 48…*

- Next, pointing in turn to each of the multiples below the number line, and then the corresponding number 1–12 above the line, say the division facts to the children, for example:
  - *12 divided by 12 is 1*
  - *24 divided by 12 is 2*
  - *36 divided by 12 is 3…*
  - *48 divided by 12 is 4 …*

Whole-class, paired or individual activities

Using the Maths Facts in the *Facts and Games* book

(continued)

- Draw children's attention to the use of colour: the multiples of 2, 4 and 8 are in red, the multiples of 3, 6 and 12 in green, and the multiples of 5 and 10 in blue. Remind children of the relationships between different multiplication tables:
  - the answers to the 4 times table are double the answers to the 2 times table, for example, $3 \times 2 = 6$ and $3 \times 4 = 12$
  - the answers to the 8 times table are double the answers to the 4 times table, for example, $3 \times 4 = 12$ and $3 \times 8 = 24$
  - the answers to the 6 times table are double the answers to the 3 times table, for example, $7 \times 3 = 21$ and $7 \times 6 = 42$
  - the answers to the 12 times table are double the answers to the 6 times table, for example, $7 \times 6 = 42$ and $7 \times 12 = 84$.
- Ensure the children realise that knowing the relationship between different multiplication tables can help them derive the answers to unknown facts.
- Also discuss with the children how knowing the multiplication tables up to 12×12, and using and applying the commutative law and inverse relationship between multiplication and division, can help them derive answers to related number facts involving:
  - multiples of 10 and 100, for example, $6 \times 12 = 72$ and $72 \div 12 = 6$, therefore $60 \times 12 = 720$, $720 \div 12 = 60$, $6 \times 120 = 720$, $720 \div 120 = 6$; $600 \times 12 = 7200$, $7200 \div 12 = 600$, $60 \times 120 = 7200$ and $7200 \div 120 = 60$
  - decimals, for example, $6 \times 12 = 72$ and $72 \div 12 = 6$, therefore $0 \cdot 6 \times 12 = 7 \cdot 2$, $6 \times 1 \cdot 2 = 7 \cdot 2$, $7 \cdot 2 \div 12 = 0 \cdot 6$ and if appropriate, $7 \cdot 2 \div 1 \cdot 2 = 6$.
- Repeat for other multiplication tables and the related facts involving multiples of 10 and 100, as well as those involving decimals.
- Conclude by hiding the PDF file, asking the children to close their copy of the *Facts and Games: Years 5 & 6* book and ask the class questions similar to the following:
  - *What is 8 multiplied by 12?*
  - *What is 84 divided by 12?*
  - *How many twelves are there in 24?*
  - *If you know that 9 multiplied by 12 is 108, what is the answer to 90 multiplied by 12? What about 900 times 12? What about 0·9 times 12?*
  - *If you know that 48 divided by 12 is 4, what is the answer to 480 divided by 12? What about 4800 divided by 12? What about 4·8 divided by 12?*

Pairs

- Provide each pair with a copy of the *Facts and Games: Years 5 & 6* book and direct their attention to the relevant number line on pages 27 and 28. Alternatively, ask the children to choose the multiplication and division facts that they know they need to develop greater fluency of.
- Children spend just two or three minutes individually using the number line to assist them in developing greater fluency of the facts.
- Children then take turns to take charge of the book and ask each other questions similar to those above, including those involving multiples of 10 and 100, as well as those involving decimals.

(continued)

Whole-class, paired or individual activities

Using the Maths Facts in the *Facts and Games* book

(continued)

 Individual

- Provide the child with a copy of the *Facts and Games: Years 5 & 6* book and direct their attention to the relevant number line on pages 27 and 28. Alternatively, ask the child to choose the multiplication and division facts that they know they need to develop greater fluency of.

- It is recommended that the child spends just five or ten minutes each time, focussing their attention on developing greater fluency of the facts.

- To provide some personal challenge, suggest the child:
  - covers the numbers (multiples) below the number line and recites the multiplication facts to themselves
  - covers the numbers 1–12 above the number line and recites the division facts to themselves
  - recalls the related facts involving multiples of 10 and 100, as well as those involving decimals.

Using the Maths Facts in the *Facts and Games* book

(continued)

Multiplication square to 12 × 12
(pages 29 and 30)

Multiples of 10 multiplication square (page 31)

Decimals multiplication square (page 32)

The square on page 29 shows the calculations (without the answers) that make up the multiplication facts up to 12 × 12. The square on page 30 shows the answers (multiples) corresponding to the multiplication calculations. These squares can be used to show that multiplication of two numbers can be done in any order (commutative). The square on page 30 can also be used to show the relationship between multiplication and division.

The square on page 31 shows the multiplication facts for the multiples of 10 from 20 to 120 up to the 12th multiple. The square on page 32 shows the multiplication facts for decimals from 0·2 to 1·2 up to the 12th multiple. Both these tables mirror the 'Multiplication square to 12 × 12' on pages 29 and 30.

The multiplication calculations and corresponding multiples for 2, 4 and 8 are in red, the calculations and multiples for 3, 6 and 12 in green, and the calculations and multiples for 5 and 10 in blue. This corresponds with the colours used on pages 19–28 and 33–43. The use of colour has been used to highlight the relationship between different multiplication tables.

How to use the Maths Facts

 Whole class

- Display the appropriate PDF file (CD-ROM / Maths Facts / Multiplication and division) and provide each child or pair with a copy of the *Facts and Games: Years 5 & 6* book and direct their attention to the two squares on pages 29 and 30.

- Begin by discussing the 'Multiplication square to 12 × 12' on page 29 with the children. Ask the children to identify different patterns and relationships in the square and discuss these with the class. Draw their attention to the row of 12 numbers at the top of the square and the column of 12 numbers down the left-hand side of the square.

- If necessary, remind the children how to use the square. Put one finger on 6 in the column of numbers down the left-hand side of the square and another finger on 8 in the row of numbers at the top of the square, and then move both fingers across and down the square until they meet at the calculation, i.e. 6 × 8.

(continued)

Using the Maths Facts in the *Facts and Games* book

(continued)

- Next, display page 30 to the children, which shows the answers (multiples) to the calculations on page 29.
- As with page 29, if necessary remind the children how to find the answer to 6 × 8.
- Repeat above several times for other calculations, moving between pages 29 and 30 as you go. As you do so, remind children of:
  - the commutative law and how, for example, 8 × 6 is the same as 6 × 8
  - the inverse relationship between multiplication and division and how to use the square to help them recall the answers to division facts
  - the use of colour to highlight the relationship between different multiplication tables:
    - ○ the answers to the 4 times table are double the answers to the 2 times table, for example, 3 × 2 = 6 and 3 × 4 = 12
    - ○ the answers to the 8 times table are double the answers to the 4 times table, for example, 3 × 4 = 12 and 3 × 8 = 24
    - ○ the answers to the 6 times table are double the answers to the 3 times table, for example, 7 × 3 = 21 and 7 × 6 = 42;
    - ○ the answers to the 12 times table are double the answers to the 6 times table, for example, 7 × 6 = 42 and 7 × 12 = 84.
- Ensure children realise that having instant recall of the multiplication tables up to 12 × 12 can help them derive answers to related multiplication and division facts. The squares on pages 31 and 32 assist in developing this understanding and recall. It is recommended that teachers introduce these squares to the children during different sessions.

Multiples of 10 multiplication square

- Draw children's attention to the 'Multiples of 10 multiplication square' on page 31 and display the relevant PDF. Discuss with the children the similarities between this square, and the two squares on pages 29 and 30.
- Highlight the following to the children:
  - The square on page 31 shows the multiplication facts for the multiples of 10 from 20 to 120 up to the 12th multiple.
  - If you know that 8 × 12 = 96 (as shown on the square on page 30), then you also know that 80 × 12 = 960 (as shown on the square on page 31).
  - Multiplication can be done in any order, so 80 × 12 = 960 and 12 × 80 = 960.
  - Multiplication is the inverse of division, so if you know that 80 × 12 = 960 you also know that 960 ÷ 80 = 12 and 960 ÷ 12 = 80.

Whole-class, paired or individual activities

Using the Maths Facts in the *Facts and Games* book

(continued)

Decimals multiplication square

- Draw children's attention to the 'Decimals multiplication square' on page 32 and display the relevant PDF. Discuss with the children the similarities between this square, and the two squares on pages 29 and 30.
- Highlight the following to the children:
  - The square on page 32 shows the multiplication facts for decimals from 0·2 to 1·2 up to the 12th multiple.
  - If you know that 8 × 12 = 96 (as shown on the square on page 30), then you also know that 0·8 × 12 = 9·6 (as shown on the square on page 32).
  - Multiplication can be done in any order, so 0·8 × 12 = 9·6 and 12 × 0·8 = 9·6.
  - Multiplication is the inverse of division, so if you know that 0·8 × 12 = 9·6 you also know that 9·6 ÷ 12 = 0·8 and if appropriate, 9·6 ÷ 1·2 = 8.

- Conclude by referring to the relevant PDF file on display, and ask the class questions similar to the following:
  - *If we know that 6 times 12 is 72, what is the answer to 60 times 12? How does the table help us check? What about 0·6 times 12?*
  - *If we know that 7 multiplied by 12 is 84, what is the answer to 84 divided by 12? What about 840 divided by 12? What about 8·4 divided by 12?*

 Pairs

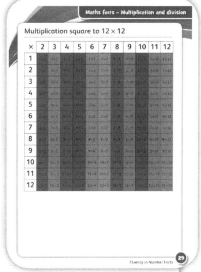

- Provide each pair with a copy of the *Facts and Games: Years 5 & 6* book. Children stand the book up so that one child is looking at page 29, while the other child is looking at page 30.
- The child looking at page 30 identifies a multiplication calculation using the row of numbers at the top of the square and the column of numbers down the left-hand side of the square and says the calculation to their partner, for example: *7 times 12*.
- The child looking at page 29 finds that calculation on the square and says the answer to their partner.
- The child looking at page 30 then says whether this answer is correct or not.
- After about five minutes, children swap roles and repeat.
- To use the square to practise and consolidate division facts, children refer to the multiplication square on page 30. They cover the numbers in the left-hand column (or top row) and take turns to ask each other division questions. They check the answer each time by removing the cover on the left-hand column (or top row).
- To use the squares on pages 31 or 32 to practise and consolidate multiplication facts involving multiples of 10 or decimals, children cover all the numbers on the coloured squares leaving only the numbers in the left-hand column and top row visible. They take turns to ask each other questions, checking the answer each time by removing the cover on the numbers on the coloured squares.

(continued)

Using the Maths Facts in the *Facts and Games* book

(continued)

 Individual

- Provide the child with a copy of the *Facts and Games: Years 5 & 6* book.

- Beginning on page 29, the child points to one of the calculations and recalls the answer. They then turn over to page 30 to check whether this answer is correct or not.

- It is recommended that the child spends just five or ten minutes each time, focussing their attention on developing greater fluency of the facts.

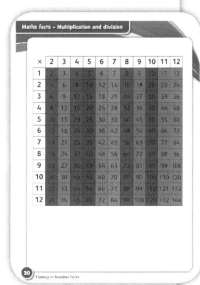

- To use the square to practise and consolidate division facts, the child uses the multiplication square on page 30. They cover the numbers in the left-hand column (or top row) and ask themselves a division question. They check the answer each time by removing the cover on the left-hand column (or top row).

- To use the squares on pages 31 or 32 to practise and consolidate multiplication facts involving multiples of 10 or decimals, the child covers all the numbers on the coloured squares leaving only the numbers in the left-hand column and top row visible. They ask themselves a question, checking the answer each time by removing the cover on the numbers on the coloured squares.

Whole-class, paired or individual activities

Using the Maths Facts in the *Facts and Games* book

(continued)

Trios for the multiplication tables to 12 × 12 (pages 33–43)

'Trios' show the relationship between the three numbers that make up a multiplication fact and the related division fact. They can be used to show that multiplication of two numbers can be done in any order (commutative) and how this law does *not* apply to division.

The trios for 2, 4 and 8 are in red, the trios for 3, 6 and 9 in green, and the trios for 5 and 10 in blue. This corresponds with the colours used on pages 19–32. The use of colour has been used to highlight the relationship between different multiplication tables.

How to use the Maths Facts

 Whole class

- Display the appropriate PDF file (CD-ROM / Maths Facts / Multiplication and division) and provide each child or pair with a copy of the *Facts and Games: Years 5 & 6* book and direct their attention to the relevant times tables and related division facts on pages 33–43.

- There are 12 sets of trios for each multiplication table, so begin by referring to each set of trios in turn, asking the children to identify different patterns and relationships between the four calculations in the trio.

- Remind the children of the following:
  - that each trio consists of only three numbers, for example, 5, 12 and 60, and that these three numbers produce four calculations: two multiplication calculations (5 × 12 = 60 and 12 × 5 = 60), and two division calculations (60 ÷ 12 = 5 and 60 ÷ 5 = 12)
  - how multiplication of two numbers can be done in any order (commutative law)
  - how the commutative law does *not* apply to division
  - the inverse relationship between multiplication and division.

- Also discuss with the children how knowing the multiplication and division facts for the multiplication tables up to 12 × 12, can help them derive answers to related number facts involving:
  - multiples of 10 and 100, for example, 5 × 12 = 60, therefore 50 × 12 = 600, 5 × 120 = 600; 500 × 12 = 6000 and 50 × 120 = 6000
  - decimals, for example, 5 × 12 = 60, therefore 0·5 × 12 = 6 and 5 × 1·2 = 6.

- Repeat for other multiplication and division facts and the related facts involving multiples of 10 and 100, as well as those involving decimals.

(continued)

Using the Maths Facts in the *Facts and Games* book

(continued)

- Conclude by hiding the PDF file, asking the children to close their copy of the *Facts and Games: Years 5 & 6* book and ask the class questions similar to the following:
  - *What is 5 times 12?*
  - *What is 4 multiplied by 12?*
  - *What is the product of 11 and 12?*
  - *12 and what other number when multiplied together make 72?*
  - *If you know that 7 times 12 is 84, what is the answer to 70 times 12? What about 7 times 120? What about 0·7 multiplied by 12?*
  - *If you know that 12 multiplied by 6 is 72, what related calculations can you tell me that involve multiples of 10 or 100? What calculations involving decimals can you tell me that use this fact?*

 Pairs

- Provide each pair with a copy of the *Facts and Games: Years 5 & 6* book and direct their attention to the relevant times tables and related division facts on pages 33–43. Alternatively, ask the children to choose the multiplication tables that they know they need to develop greater fluency of.
- Children take turns to choose one of the trios and place their hand / fingers over the list of four calculations.
- Referring to the three numbers on the triangle, the other child says the two multiplication and two division number facts.
- Once they have done this, the child covering the facts removes their hand / fingers to reveal the four calculations.
- Vary the activity by asking children to ask each other questions involving multiples of 10 and 100, as well as those involving decimals.

 Individual

- Provide the child with a copy of the *Facts and Games: Years 5 & 6* book and direct their attention to the relevant times tables and related division facts on pages 33–43. Alternatively, ask the child to choose the multiplication tables that they know they need to develop greater fluency of.
- It is recommended that the child spends just five or ten minutes each time, focussing their attention on developing greater fluency of the facts.
- To provide some personal challenge, as for the paired activity above, suggest the child:
  - places their hand / fingers over the list of four calculations and recites the facts to themselves
  - recalls the related facts involving multiples of 10 and 100, as well as those involving decimals.

Swimming pool

Multiplication

Division

Objective

- Recall multiplication and division facts for multiplication tables up to 12 × 12

Pupil resources

- *Fluency in Number Facts: Facts and Games: Years 5 & 6* book pages 68 and 69 (per pair); PDFs:

Paired games and activities → Paired games from the *Facts and Games: Years 5 & 6* book

- 2 different buttons: 1 for each player (per pair)
- 1–12 dice (per pair)
- 20 counters (per pair)

Note

- For 'Swimming pool: Multiplication', remind the children that the same multiple may appear in several multiplication tables and that they can put their button on any of these, for example, if they roll 6 and 4, they can cover the number 24 in the 2 times table, 3 times table, 4 times table, 6 times table, 8 times table or 12 times table.

Variations

- Children play the games in groups of three. You need three different buttons: one for each player.

Swimming pool: Multiplication

 or

- Do not use the buttons. Use 30 counters. Take turns to roll the dice twice, multiply the two numbers together, and place a counter on the answer in the pool. The winner is the first player to complete a line of three counters. A line can go vertically, horizontally or diagonally.

- Children play the game individually using 15 counters. Can the child complete a line of three counters before they use all 15 counters? A line can go vertically, horizontally or diagonally.

A day at the beach

Multiples of 10
Multiples of 100

Objective

- Multiply multiples of 10 and 100 by a 1-digit number mentally, drawing upon known multiplication facts

Pupil resources

 →

Paired games and activities → Paired games from the *Facts and Games: Years 5 & 6 book*

- *Fluency in Number Facts: Facts and Games: Years 5 & 6* book pages 70 and 71 (per pair); PDFs:
- 0–9 dice (per pair)
- pencil and paperclip (for the spinner) (per pair)
- 12 counters (per pair)

Note

- Before the children play the game, ensure that they are familiar with how to use the spinner (see *Facts and Games: Years 5 & 6* book page 80).

Variations

A day at the beach: Multiples of 10

 or

Divide a 3-digit multiple of 10 by a 2-digit multiple of 10 mentally, drawing upon known multiplication facts

- Do not use the dice or pencil and paperclip for the spinner. Use 32 counters. Cover all the numbers on the blue umbrella with a counter. Take turns to remove a counter, say the division calculation using the number under the counter and any one of the numbers on the blue beach ball. If you can, cover that number on the beach ball. That number cannot be used again. If you cannot say a calculation using the number you have uncovered and one of the remaining numbers on the beach ball, you must keep that counter. The winner is the player with fewest counters once all the numbers on the beach ball are covered.

A day at the beach: Multiples of 100

 or

Divide a 4-digit multiple of 100 by a 3-digit multiple of 100 mentally, drawing upon known multiplication facts

- Play the game as described above, using the red and white umbrella and beach ball.

A day at the beach: Multiples of 10

- Children play the game individually. They decide whether they will have the numbers on the blue strips of the umbrella or the white strips. If the product of each calculation appears on the umbrella, cover the number with a counter. Can the child cover six of the numbers on their chosen strips before they run out of counters?

A day at the beach: Multiples of 100

- Children play the game individually as described above, deciding whether they will have the numbers on the red strips of the umbrella or the white strips.

Multiples of Australia

Multiples of 10
Multiples of 10 and 100

Objective

- Multiply pairs of multiples of 10 and 100 mentally, drawing upon known multiplication facts

Pupil resources

- *Fluency in Number Facts: Facts and games: Years 5 & 6* book pages 72 and 73 (per pair); PDFs:

Paired games and activities → Paired games from the *Facts and Games: Years 5 & 6* book

- pencil and paperclip (for the spinner) (per pair)
- 16 counters: 8 of one colour, 8 of another colour (per pair)

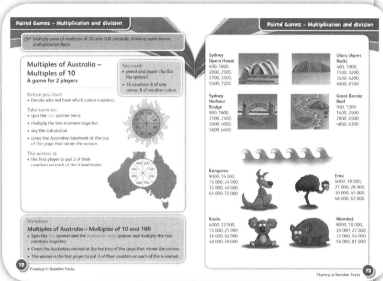

Note

- Before the children play the game, ensure that they are familiar with how to use the spinner (see *Facts and Games: Years 5 & 6* book page 80).

Variations

- Children play the game in groups of three. You need 24 counters: eight each of three different colours.

Multiples of Australia: Multiples of 10

- Children play the game individually. If there are already two counters on a landmark, discard a counter. Can the child get two counters on each landmark before all the 16 counters are used up?

Multiples of Australia: Multiples of 10 and 100

- Children play the game individually. If there are already two counters on an animal, discard a counter. Can the child get two counters on each animal before all the 16 counters are used up?

Movie time

Objective

- Multiply a 2-digit number by a 1-digit number

Pupil resources

- *Fluency in Number Facts: Facts and Games: Years 5 & 6* book pages 74 and 75 (per pair); PDFs:

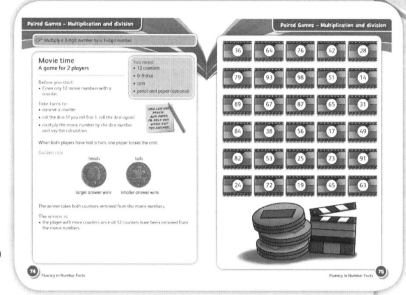

Paired games and activities → Paired games from the *Facts and Games: Years 5 & 6* book

- 12 counters (per pair)
- 0–9 dice (per pair)
- coin (per pair)
- pencil and paper (optional) (per pair)

Variations

- Children play the game in groups of three. You need 18 counters. Before you start cover 18 movie numbers with a counter. On the coin toss: heads – largest number wins; tails – smallest number wins.

 or

Divide a 2-digit number by a 1-digit number mentally, drawing upon known facts.

- Do not use the coin. Divide the movie number by the dice number. The player with the smaller / smallest remainder wins that round and takes both (or all three) counters. If all players have the same remainder, discard the counters.

The remainders in the tower

Objective

- Divide a 2-digit number by a 1-digit number

Pupil resources

- *Fluency in Number Facts: Facts and Games: Years 5 & 6* book pages 76 and 77 (per pair); PDFs:

Paired games and activities → Paired games from the *Facts and Games: Years 5 & 6* book

- 12 counters (per pair)
- 0–9 dice (per pair)

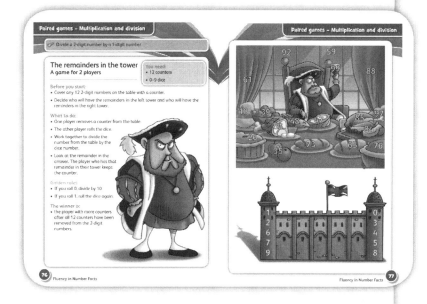

Variations

- Children play the game in groups of three.

 Multiply a 2-digit number by a 1-digit number mentally, drawing upon known facts

Before you start

- Cover any 12 numbers on the table with a counter.
- Decide who will have the numbers in the left tower and who will have the numbers in the right tower.

What to do

- One player removes a counter from the table, for example, 47.
- The other player rolls the dice (if you roll 0 or 1 roll the dice again), for example, 8.
- Work together to multiply the dice number by the number from the table, i.e. 376.
- The player with the tens digit of the product in their tower keeps the counter, for example, 7.

The winner is:

- the player with more counters once all 12 counters have been removed from the table.

- Children play the game individually. They decide which of the two towers will belong to them. If the remainder is in their tower, they put a counter on their side of the castle. If the remainder is in the other tower, they put a counter on that side of the castle. Do they have more counters on their side of the castle than on the other side, once all 12 counters have been moved?

Multiplication and division facts

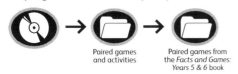 Robot wars

Objective

- Multiply 1-digit numbers with up to two decimal places by whole numbers

Pupil resources

- *Fluency in Number Facts: Facts and Games: Years 5 & 6* book pages 78 and 79 (per pair); PDFs:

 → →

Paired games and activities → Paired games from the *Facts and Games: Years 5 & 6* book

- button (per pair)
- 0–9 dice (per pair)
- 10 counters (per pair)
- pencil and paper (optional) (per pair)

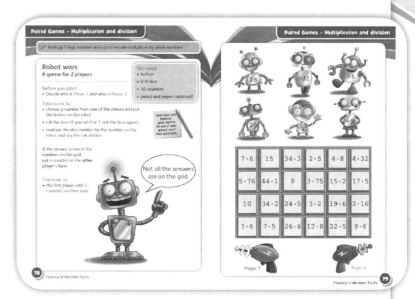

Variations

 or

- Do not use the button or dice. Cover the numbers on the robots with a counter. Take turns to remove a counter. The first player to say a multiplication calculation using the robot number, where the product is on the grid, keeps the counter. The winner is the player with more counters once all the counters have been removed from the robots.

- Children play the game individually. If the product of the dice number and the robot number is on the grid, they put a counter on the laser for Player 2. If the product is not on the grid, they put a counter on the laser for Player 1. They win if, after all ten counters have been used, the laser for Player 2 has more counters on it than the laser for Player 1.

Times-table practice

Objectives

- Recall and use multiplication facts for multiplication tables up to 12 × 12
- Multiply numbers mentally drawing upon known facts

Pupil resources

- 1–12 dice (per pair)
- 20 counters: 10 counters for each player (per pair)
- container (per pair)

What to do

- Decide which multiplication table you want the children to practice, for example, 8 multiplication table.
- Children take turns to roll the dice.
- Each child multiplies the dice number by 8.
- The first child to call out the correct answer places one of their counters into the container.
- The winner is the first player to place all their counters into the container.

Variations

- Ask the children to multiply the dice number by a multiple of 10 from 20 to 120, i.e. 20 / 30 / 40 / 50 / 60 / 70 / 80 / 90 / 100 / 110 or 120.
- Ask the children to multiply the dice number by a decimal from 0·2 to 1·2, i.e. 0·2 / 0·3 / 0·4 / 0·5 / 0·6 / 0·7 / 0·8 / 0·9 / 1·1 or 1·2.

Win the counters

Objectives

- Recall and use multiplication facts for multiplication tables up to 12 × 12
- Multiply numbers mentally drawing upon known facts

Pupil resources

Whole-class games and activities → Hands-on game boards

- 'Hands-on: Multiples of …' game board (per pair)
- 1–12 dice (per pair)
- 20 counters (per pair)

What to do

- Decide which multiplication table you want the children to practise, for example, 8 multiplication table, and provide them with the appropriate game board, i.e. 'Hands-on Multiples of 8' game board.
- Each player puts their index finger on one of the hands at the bottom of the game board.
- One child rolls the dice, for example, 6.
- Both children multiply the dice number by the multiplication table they are practising, for example, 8 multiplication table: 6 × 8 = 48.
- The first player to point to the correct answer on the game board wins a counter.
- The winner is the player with more counters once all 20 counters have been won.

Variations

- Provide each pair with a copy of the 'Hands-on: Multiples of 20 / 30 / 40 / 50 / 60 / 70 / 80 / 90 / 100 / 110 or 120' game board.
- Provide each pair with a copy of the 'Hands-on: Multiples of 0·2 / 0·3 / 0·4 / 0·5 / 0·6 / 0·7 / 0·8 / 0·9 / 1·1 or 1·2' game board.

Cover the multiples

Objectives

- Recall and use multiplication facts for multiplication tables up to 12 × 12
- Multiply numbers mentally drawing upon known facts

Pupil resources

Whole-class games and activities → Hands-on game boards

- 'Hands-on: Multiples of …' game board (per pair)
- 1–12 dice (per pair)
- 20 counters: 10 of one colour, 10 of another colour (per pair)

What to do

- Decide which multiplication table you want the children to practise, for example, 8 multiplication table, and provide them with the appropriate game-board, i.e. 'Hands-on Multiples of 8' game board.
- Children decide who will have which colour counters.
- Children take turns to:
  - roll the dice, for example, 7
  - multiply the dice number by the multiplication table they are practising, for example, 8 multiplication table, and say the answer, i.e. 56.
- If the answer is correct, they place one of their counters on that number on the game board.
- If the number is already covered, they miss that turn.
- The winner is the player with more counters on the game board once all the numbers have a counter on them.

Variations

- Provide each pair with a copy of the 'Hands-on: Multiples of 20 / 30 / 40 / 50 / 60 / 70 / 80 / 90 / 100 / 110 or 120' game board.
- Provide each pair with a copy of the 'Hands-on: Multiples of 0·2 / 0·3 / 0·4 / 0·5 / 0·6 / 0·7 / 0·8 / 0·9 / 1·1 or 1·2' game board.

Stack them up

Objectives

- Recall and use multiplication facts for multiplication tables up to 12 × 12
- Multiply numbers mentally drawing upon known facts

Pupil resources

Whole-class games and activities → Hands-on game boards

- 'Hands-on: Multiples of …' game board (per pair)
- 1–12 dice (per pair)
- 20 counters: 10 of one colour, 10 of another colour (per pair)

What to do

- Decide which multiplication table you want the children to practise, for example, 8 multiplication table, and provide them with the appropriate game board, i.e. 'Hands-on: Multiples of 8' game board.
- Children decide who will have which colour counters.
- Children take turns to:
  - roll the dice, for example, 6
  - multiply the dice number by the multiplication table they are practising, for example, 8 multiplication table, and say the answer, i.e. 48.
- If their answer is correct, they place one of their counters on that number (but making sure not to cover the number) on the game board.
- If the number already has a counter on it, either with one of their own counters, or one the other player's counters, they place their counter on top of the pile.
- The player whose colour counter is on top 'owns' the pile.
- Children keep going, taking turns, until each player has put their ten counters on the game board.
- Each player then carefully removes all the piles where the top counter is their colour.
- Each player then counts how many counters they have altogether (of both colours).
- The winner is the player with more counters.

Variations

- Provide each pair with a copy of the 'Hands-on: Multiples of 20 / 30 / 40 / 50 / 60 / 70 / 80 / 90 / 100 / 110 or 120' game board.
- Provide each pair with a copy of the 'Hands-on: Multiples of 0·2 / 0·3 / 0·4 / 0·5 / 0·6 / 0·7 / 0·8 / 0·9 / 1·1 or 1·2' game board.

Multiplication and division Flip Facts cards

Objective

- Recall and use multiplication and division facts for multiplication tables up to 12 × 12

Resources

Individual activities → Flip Facts cards → Multiplication and division

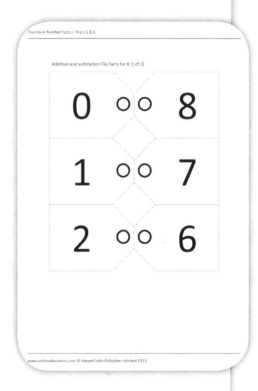

- 'Multiplication and division Flip Facts cards'
- scissors
- glue
- hole punch
- small piece of string or paper fastener

What to do

- Cut out the cards along the dashed lines.
- Fold each card along the dotted lines to form two-sided cards.
- Glue together the back of each card.
- Punch a hole in the centre of each card.
- Arrange the cards in order with the smallest number on top.
- Fasten the set of cards together with string or a paper fastener.

To practise the multiplication facts for the 8 multiplication table

- Use the 'Multiplication and division Flip Facts cards for 8'.
- Start with the 1 card on top.
- Ask yourself: *1 multiplied by 8 is…?* (8) Turn over the card to check. *2 multiplied by 8 is…?* (16) Turn over the card to check. *3 multiplied by 8 is…?* (24) Turn over the card to check.
- Continue until you reach the card showing 12 and ask: *12 multiplied by 8 is…?* (96).
- Repeat several times, quickening the pace as you go.

(continued)

Multiplication and division facts

To practise the division facts for the 8 multiplication table

- Use the 'Multiplication and division Flip Facts cards for 8'.
- Start with the 96 card on top.
- Ask yourself: *96 divided by 8 is…?* (12) Turn over the card to check. *88 divided by 8 is…?* (11) Turn over the card to check. *80 divided by 8 is…?* (10) Turn over the card to check.
- Continue until you reach the card showing 8 and ask: *8 divided by 8 is…?* (1)
- Repeat several times, quickening the pace as you go.

- Children spend just five or ten minutes each time, focussing their attention on learning the multiplication and division facts off by heart.

Variations

- Use the 'Multiplication and division Flip Facts cards' for 2, 3, 4, 5, 6, 7, 9, 10, 11 and 12 to practise the other multiplication and division facts for multiplication tables up to 12 × 12.
- Use the 'Multiplication and division Flip Facts cards' for 0·2, 0·3, 0·4, 0·5, 0·6, 0·7, 0·8, 0·9, 1·1 and 1·2 to practise the related multiplication facts involving decimals. If appropriate, use these Flip Facts cards to practise division. However be aware that children will be dividing a decimal by a decimal, for example, 5·6 ÷ 0·8 = 7, and that for some this may not be appropriate.

Number and place value

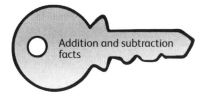
Addition and subtraction facts

Multiplication and division facts

Sit down, stand up

Objectives

- Order and compare numbers up to 10 000 000 and determine the value of each digit
- Round any whole number to a required degree of accuracy
- Order and compare numbers with up to three decimal places
- Identify the value of each digit to three decimal places
- Round decimals with two decimal places to the nearest whole number and to one decimal place
- Add and subtract numbers mentally with increasingly large numbers and decimals
- Recall and use multiplication and division facts for multiplication tables up to 12 × 12
- Multiply and divide numbers mentally drawing upon known facts
- Multiply and divide whole numbers and those involving decimals by 10, 100 and 1000

Teacher resources

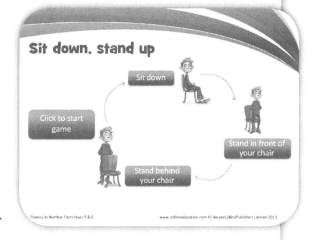

Whole-class games and activities → PowerPoint slides

- 'Sit down, stand up'

Pupil resources

- none

What to do

- Explain to the children that this a game of honesty.
- Display the first 'Sit down, stand up' slide:
  - sit down
  - stand in front of your chair
  - stand behind your chair
- All the children start the game by sitting.
- Ask the class an appropriate question, for example: *What is 45 divided by 100?*
- Ask a child for the answer, i.e. 0·45.
- All the children that worked out the correct answer stand up in front of their chair.
- Continue asking questions.
- Each time a child works out the correct answer to a question, they move to a different position following the order on the slide.
- If a child works out an incorrect answer to a question they stay in their current position.
- Continue asking questions until there are some children sitting down, some children standing in front of their chair and other children standing behind their chair.
- Finally, in rapid succession display slides 2 to 7 (which form a continual loop) eventually stopping on one of the slides.
- All the children in the position displayed on the slide are the winners.

Whole-class games and activities

Number and place value

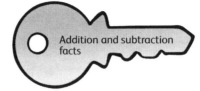
Addition and subtraction facts

Multiplication and division facts

Target boards

Objectives

- Read, order and compare numbers up to 10 000 000 and determine the value of each digit
- Round any whole number to a required degree of accuracy
- Read, order and compare numbers with up to three decimal places
- Identify the value of each digit to three decimal places
- Round decimals with two decimal places to the nearest whole number and to one decimal place
- Add and subtract numbers mentally with increasingly large numbers and decimals
- Recall and use multiplication and division facts for multiplication tables up to 12 × 12
- Multiply and divide numbers mentally drawing upon known facts
- Multiply and divide whole numbers and those involving decimals by 10, 100 and 1000

Teacher resources

Whole-class games and activities → PowerPoint slides

- 'Target boards'

Pupil resources

- none

What to do

- Display the first 'Target boards' slide.
- Ask questions similar to the following:
  - *Which number has 4 tens, 8 units and 6 hundreds?*
  - *Tell me the number that is between 2 and 3?*
  - *Which number rounds to 400?*
  - *Which number has two decimal places?*
  - *Which two numbers make a total of 744?*
  - *Which two numbers have a difference of 68?*
  - *Which two numbers when multiplied together equal 3600?*
  - *Which two numbers when the larger number is divided by the smaller number have an answer of 2?*
- Ask children to point and say different calculations and expressions using the numbers and symbols on the board, for example, 4800 ÷ 1000 = 4·8, $\frac{1}{2}$ × 720 = 360.

Target boards

<	5341	12	$\frac{1}{2}$	6·45
10	78	648	÷	720
7	$\frac{1}{4}$	8	0.9	×
+	2·8	>	4800	–
$\frac{1}{5}$	24	16 456	360	1000

Fluency in Number Facts Years 5 & 6   www.collinseducation.com © HarperCollins Publishers Limited 2013

Variations

- Use the second 'Target boards' slide.
- Change the content in either of the target boards.
- Present the children with a target board where some of the boxes are empty. Ask the children to suggest the content for the empty boxes on the target board.

 Number and place value

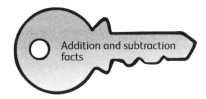 Addition and subtraction facts

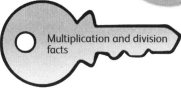 Multiplication and division facts

Hand me your cards

Objectives

- Recognise the place value of each digit in whole numbers and decimals (Game 1)
- Order and compare whole numbers and decimals (Game 2)
- Multiply and divide whole numbers and decimals by 10, 100 and 1000 (Game 3)
- Add and subtract numbers mentally, including multiples of 100 and 1000 (Game 4)
- Add and subtract numbers mentally, including a 3-digit number and a 2-digit number (Game 5)
- Add and subtract decimals mentally, U·t ± U·t and U·th ± U·th (Game 6)
- Recall multiplication and division facts for multiplication tables up to 12 × 12, and use them to derive related multiplication and division facts involving multiples of 10 and 100 (Game 7)
- Multiply and divide numbers mentally, including a 2-digit number by a 1-digit number (Game 8)
- Recall multiplication and division facts for multiplication tables up to 12 × 12, and use them to derive related multiplication and division facts involving decimals (Game 9)

Teacher resources

Whole-class games and activities → Hand me your cards

- 'Hand me your cards' Teacher's call card

Pupil resources

Whole-class games and activities → Hand me your cards

- 'Hand me your cards' (the white and grey answer cards, ideally printed onto card)

What to do

- Choose the appropriate game for the objective(s) you want the children to practise and consolidate (see above).
- Arrange the class into four teams.
- Separately shuffle and distribute the white and grey answer cards. Each team must have nine answer cards – either all white cards or all grey answer cards. Depending on the number of children in the class, some children may have more than one card. Cards with the **Challenge 1** icon denote the answer to an easier question. Cards with the **Challenge 3** icon denote the answer to a more difficult question.
- Read out the 'What to say' questions from the Teacher's call card (but not the answers!). Read the questions from the top to the bottom of each column, asking all the questions in the left-hand column first, then all the questions in the right-hand column. Note that there are two answer cards for each number, to ensure there is competition to 'be the first' to call out the answer.

(continued)

- The first child who has the correct answer on their card, and who calls out this answer, hands their card to the teacher. Team members may assist each other, but only the child that is holding the card can call out the answer.
- Once a child has handed in his/her card(s), they may still assist their team members with the remaining cards. As before, however, he/she is not allowed to call out the answer to the teacher – only the child that is holding the card can call it out.
- Continue asking the questions from the Teacher's call card.
- The winner is the first team with all their answer cards handed in.
- Continue to play the game to see which teams come second and third.

Variations

- Arrange the class into different number of teams:
  - two teams, giving each team 18 cards
  - three teams, giving each team 12 cards (**Note:** One team will have six white answer cards and six grey answer cards)
  - six teams, giving each team six cards.
- Read the questions from the bottom to the top of each column, asking the questions in the left-hand column first, then the questions in the right-hand column. Or ask the questions in the right-hand column first.
- Put the answer cards in the middle of the table so the group can help each other from the start.

Whole-class games and activities

Number and place value

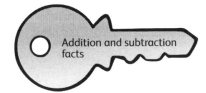
Addition and subtraction facts

Multiplication and division facts

Loop cards

Objectives

- Recognise the place value of each digit in whole numbers and decimals (Game 1)
- Order and compare whole numbers and decimals (Game 2)
- Multiply and divide whole numbers and decimals by 10, 100 and 1000 (Game 3)
- Add and subtract numbers mentally, including multiples of 100 and 1000 (Game 4)
- Add and subtract numbers mentally, including a 3-digit number and a 2-digit number (Game 5)
- Add and subtract decimals mentally, U·t ± U·t and U·th ± U·th (Game 6)
- Recall multiplication and division facts for multiplication tables up to 12 × 12, and use them to derive related multiplication and division facts involving multiples of 10 and 100 (Game 7)
- Multiply and divide numbers mentally, including a 2-digit number by a 1-digit number (Game 8)
- Recall multiplication and division facts for multiplication tables up to 12 × 12, and use them to derive related multiplication and division facts involving decimals (Game 9)

Teacher resources

- none

Pupil resources

- 'Loop cards' (ideally printed onto card)

Whole-class games and activities → Loop cards

What to do

- Choose the appropriate game for the objective(s) you want the children to practise and consolidate (see above).
- Shuffle the cards and hand them out to the children. Every card must be used, so if necessary give some children more than one card. Cards with the **Challenge 1** icon denote the answer to an easier question. Cards with the **Challenge 3** icon denote the answer to a more difficult question.
- Decide who will start the game (the game can begin with any card).
- The first player reads aloud the text on the right-hand side of the card, for example: *Who has 10 more than 30?*
- The rest of the children work out the answer, and the child who has the correct answer on the left-hand side of their card reads it out, for example: *I have 40.* If the answer is correct, that player then reads the text on the right-hand side of their card, for example: *Who has 10 less than 176?*
- The game continues in this way.
- The game ends when the child who started the game reads out the answer on the left-hand side of their card.

Variation

- To encourage a brisk pace and increase fluency, use a timer and display the 'time to beat'.

Number and place value

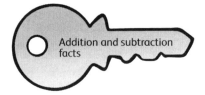

Addition and subtraction facts

Multiplication and division facts

Around the room

Objectives

- Count forwards or backwards in steps
- Order and compare numbers up to 10 000 000 and determine the value of each digit
- Round any whole number to a required degree of accuracy
- Order and compare numbers with up to three decimal places
- Identify the value of each digit to three decimal places
- Round decimals with two decimal places to the nearest whole number and to one decimal place
- Add and subtract numbers mentally with increasingly large numbers and decimals
- Recall and use multiplication and division facts for multiplication tables up to 12 × 12
- Multiply and divide numbers mentally drawing upon known facts
- Multiply and divide whole numbers and those involving decimals by 10, 100 and 1000

Teacher resources

- none

Pupil resources

- none

What to do

- Children either sit in a circle or at their tables as long as there is a logical 'path' from one child/table to the next.
- Ask one child to go and stand behind the child who is sitting next to them.
- Ask an appropriate question to these two children, for example: *What is the next number in this pattern: 125, 150, 175, 200…? What is the value of the 3 in 4·32? Which is larger: 5·42 or 5·24? What is 562 rounded to the nearest multiple of 10? What is 364 add 70? What is 9 multiplied by 12? What is 5·3 multiplied by 100?*
- If the child who is standing calls out the correct answer first, they move and stand behind the next child.
- If the child that is sitting calls out the correct answer first, they stand up and go behind the next child. The child that was just standing sits in the place of the child they were just standing behind.
- The game continues in this way around the room.
- When you have gone around the class say: *All change!* and children go back to their original positions.

 Number and place value

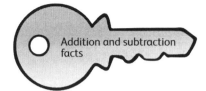 Addition and subtraction facts

 Multiplication and division facts

One name left

Objectives

- Count forwards or backwards in steps
- Order and compare numbers up to 10 000 000 and determine the value of each digit
- Round any whole number to a required degree of accuracy
- Order and compare numbers with up to three decimal places
- Identify the value of each digit to three decimal places
- Round decimals with two decimal places to the nearest whole number and to one decimal place
- Add and subtract numbers mentally with increasingly large numbers and decimals
- Recall and use multiplication and division facts for multiplication tables up to 12 × 12
- Multiply and divide numbers mentally drawing upon known facts
- Multiply and divide whole numbers and those involving decimals by 10, 100 and 1000

Teacher resources

- small box or container

Pupil resources

- small slip of paper or card (per child)
- pencil (per child)

What to do

- Ask the children to write their name on the small slip of paper or card and fold it in half.
- Collect the slips and put them into the box or container.
- Choose two names from the box.
- Ask these two children to stand.
- Ask an appropriate question to these two children, for example: *What is the next number in this pattern: 1·2, 2·4, 3·6, 4·8…? What is the value of the 7 in 571 283? Which is larger: 4·56 or 5·23? What is 7·8 rounded to the nearest whole number? What is 3·3 add 0·8? What is 7 multiplied by 0·4? What is 84 divided by 1000?*
- For the child who answers correctly first, put their slip of paper into a 'still in' pile. For the child who answers incorrectly, or is beaten on speed by the other child, put their card in an 'out' pile.
- Continue choosing two names from the box and asking a question.
- When all the names have been chosen from the box, put the children's names that are in the 'still in' pile back into the box.
- Continue the game as before, choosing two names, asking a question and putting the names into 'still in' and 'out' piles.
- Continue the game until only two children, then finally one child is left.

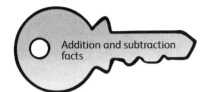 Addition and subtraction facts

 Multiplication and division facts

Whispers

Objectives

- Add and subtract numbers mentally with increasingly large numbers and decimals
- Recall and use multiplication and division facts for multiplication tables up to 12 × 12
- Multiply and divide numbers mentally drawing upon known facts
- Multiply and divide whole numbers and those involving decimals by 10, 100 and 1000

Teacher resources

- small slip of paper or card with an appropriate question written on it, for example: 76 + 50 = , 9 × 5 = , 120 ÷ 10 = …

Pupil resources

- none

What to do

- Arrange the class into two or three teams. Ideally, there should be the same number of children in each team.
- Each team stands or sits in a line.
- Secretly show the first child in each team the slip of paper or card showing an appropriate question written on it, for example: 76 + 50 = .
- When the first child in each team has seen the slip of paper say *Go!*
- The first child then works out the answer to the question and thinks of a different question that has the same answer, for example: 130 – 4. They then whisper this calculation to the second child in the line.
- The second child works out the answer, thinks of a different question with the same answer and whispers this calculation to the third child in the line.
- The activity continues as described above.
- When the last child in each team has worked out the answer to the question they are given, they call out the answer. Does the last child's answer match the original question on the slip of paper? If so, this is a winning team.

Variation

- An easier version is to show the first child in each team a number, which teams then whisper to each other.

Number and place value

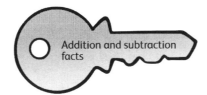
Addition and subtraction facts

Multiplication and division facts

Folding numbers

Objectives

- Count forwards or backwards in steps
- Order and compare numbers up to 10 000 000 and determine the value of each digit
- Round any whole number to a required degree of accuracy
- Add and subtract numbers mentally with increasingly large numbers
- Recall and use multiplication and division facts for multiplication tables up to 12 × 12
- Multiply and divide numbers mentally drawing upon known facts
- Multiply and divide whole numbers and those involving decimals by 10, 100 and 1000 (whole number answers only)

Teacher resources

- none

Pupil resources

- *The first time you do this activity:* coloured pencils, and/or felt-tips; sheet of A4 paper (per child and yourself)

Note to the teacher

- This activity is not just about children answering mathematical questions. More importantly, it is about encouraging children to *ask* mathematical questions.

What to do – *The first time you do this activity*

- Provide each child, and yourself, with a sheet of A4 paper and each group with some coloured pencils and/or felt-tips.
- Demonstrate and ask the children to:
  - place their sheet of paper in the landscape position on the table in front of them
  - write their name in large writing in the middle of the sheet of paper.
- Demonstrate and ask the children to:
  - fold their sheet of paper in half, side to side (it doesn't matter whether the writing is on the inside or the outside of the fold)
  - fold their sheet of paper a second time, top to bottom
  - fold their sheet of paper a third time, side to side
  - fold their sheet of paper a fourth time, top to bottom.

(continued)

Folding numbers

(continued)

- Demonstrate and ask the children to open out their sheet of paper to the blank side (not the side that has their name written on it). There should 16 small rectangles.

- Demonstrate and ask the children to use the coloured pencils and/or felt-tips to neatly write, in large writing, each of the digits 0 to 9, in any order, one digit in each small rectangle. Then in the six remaining empty rectangles, to repeat any six of the digits, for example,

- Once all the children have done this, ask them to carefully look at the numbers on their sheet.

- Demonstrate to the children how the sheet of paper can be folded to show different 1-digit, 2-digit and 3-digit numbers.

7

8	1

5
4

3	8	7

4
5
7

Folding numbers

(continued)

- Next, ask the children to fold their sheet of paper to show you the number 6.
- Repeat several times asking questions similar to the following until the children are confident in folding their sheet of paper in different ways to display different 1-digit, 2-digit, 3-digit and 4-digit numbers.
  - *Show me a number greater than 157.*
  - *Show me any 3-digit odd number.*
  - *Show me an even number less than 500.*
- Once children are confident in using their 'Folding numbers' sheet, demonstrate the following to the class, asking a confident child to come out to the front to be your partner:
  - Look at the child's 'Folding numbers' sheet and ask them a question similar to those above where the answer can be displayed on their 'Folding numbers' sheet.
  - Once the child has successfully done this, ask them to carefully look at your 'Folding numbers' sheet and to ask you a question where the answer can be displayed on your 'Folding numbers' sheet.
  - Repeat if necessary, being sure to demonstrate more open-ended types of questions to the class.
- Once children are familiar with this, arrange them into pairs.
- Tell the children to take turns in asking each other questions where the answer can be displayed on their partners 'Folding numbers' sheet. Remind the children that they need to think carefully about what questions to ask, as their partner must be able to show the answer on their 'Folding numbers' sheet.
- After a sufficient length of time, bring the class back together again and discuss with the children the range of questions that they asked. It is important to elicit from the children the difference between a 'poor' question, for example: *Can you show me the number 542?*, and a 'good' question, for example: *Can you show me a number between 384 and 431?*
- Keep the 'Folding numbers' sheets for when you revisit the activity.

What to do – *Revisiting the activity*

- Ask the children to look at their 'Folding numbers' sheets again.
- Ask pairs to take turns in asking each other questions where the answer can be displayed on their partners 'Folding numbers' sheet. Remind the children that they need to think carefully about what questions to ask, as their partner must be able to show the answer on their 'Folding numbers' sheet.
- After a sufficient length of time, bring the class back together again and briefly discuss the activity with the children.
- Keep the 'Folding numbers' sheets for the next time you revisit the activity.

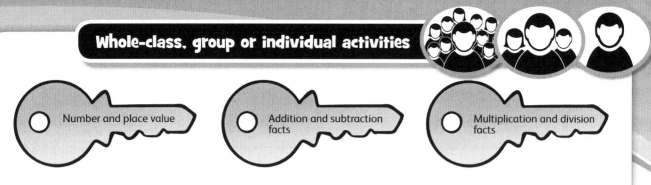

Whole-class, group or individual activities

Number and place value

Addition and subtraction facts

Multiplication and division facts

Written activities

Objectives

- Read, write, order and compare numbers up to 10 000 000
- Read, write, order and compare numbers with up to three decimal places
- Add and subtract numbers mentally with increasingly large numbers and decimals
- Recall and use multiplication and division facts for multiplication tables up to 12 × 12
- Multiply and divide numbers mentally drawing upon known facts
- Multiply and divide whole numbers and those involving decimals by 10, 100 and 1000

Teacher resources

Written activities

- scissors

Pupil resources

- Written activities sheet (per child)
- pencil (per child)

Introduction

Fluency in Number Facts: Facts and Games Years 5 & 6 includes a set of Written activities, presented as templates. They are aimed at providing children with further practice and consolidation and also at offering teachers a means of assessing individual children's proficiency in number. They can be used with the whole class, specific groups or individual children.

Although designed to be reproduced onto sheets of A4 paper, many of the templates show the same type of activity presented three times with the following icons used to allow for differentiation: **Challenge 1** (easy), **Challenge 2** (average) and **Challenge 3** (challenging). The intention is that once the teacher has filled in and copied the template that these are then cut into smaller pieces of paper for the children to complete. However, even for those templates that do not include these differentiation icons, these Written activities can also be adapted easily to meet a range of abilities. It is important therefore that these Written activities are viewed as generic worksheets that teachers fill in and adapt in order to meet the different needs and abilities of their children.

It is envisaged that, whether it be one of the full A4 activities (for example, '16 calculations', '49 calculations' or '100 calculations') or one of the activities that are presented to the children on a smaller piece of paper (for example, 'Across and up', 'Calculation boxes' or 'Dice calculations'), each Written activity should take no longer than ten minutes for the children to complete. Alternatively, to encourage speed and recall, set the children to work, and as they finish the activity they raise their hand and you tell them how long it took them to complete it.

It is recommended that children do the same type of activity (perhaps even involving the same numbers) on two or three consecutive days. This way, the majority of children will see themselves making progress over the two or three days, thus providing greater encouragement and self-motivation.

What to do

- Choose an appropriate Written activity for the whole class, specific groups or individual children, taking careful consideration of the different needs and abilities of the children.

- Fill in the template on screen, then name this version and save it to use again later on. Alternatively, print one copy of the template and fill it in by hand. Detailed guidance regarding possible differentiated content (**Challenge 1** **Challenge 2** **Challenge 3**) to use for each of the templates is given below on pages 149–169.

- Once filled in, photocopy as many copies as is required for the number of children you want to complete the Written activity. If required, cut the sheets into two or three smaller strips of paper.

- Distribute the activities to the children taking care to provide each child with the appropriate differentiated version of the activity. Also ensure that each child has a sharpened pencil!

- If it is the first time that children are doing one of the Written activities, spend time explaining how to do the activity. If appropriate, display the saved template on the interactive whiteboard (IWB) to help with the explanation.

- Allow the children approximately ten minutes to complete the activity or set the activity as a timed exercise.

- Once the children have finished, immediately mark the activity. You may want to mark the activity with the children's help, asking children to mark their own sheet or swapping and marking someone else's sheet.

- Be sure to discuss the results of the activity with the children, asking them which questions they found easy, which they found more difficult, and also referring to specific questions, asking them how they worked out the answer. This should provide some excellent data to help identify common errors or misconceptions that children may have. You can then either follow on with some brief impromptu teaching, assisting children to overcome the errors or misconceptions or, alternatively, keep this information in mind for some further teaching at a later date.

- And finally…remember to repeat the same type of activity (perhaps even involving the same numbers) on two or three consecutive days.

Whole-class, group or individual activities

Order the numbers

Number and place value

Notes for the teacher

- Children need to be familiar with the traditional 1–100 number square in order to complete this activity successfully.

- The second **Challenge 1** example on page 149 as well as the **Challenge 2** and **Challenge 3** examples, are all sections from number squares other than a 1–100 number square. Children also need to be familiar with these types of number squares in order to complete these grids successfully.

Challenge 1 10–1000 multiples of 10 number square

10	20	30	40	50	60	70	80	90	100
110	120	130	140	150	160	170	180	190	200
210	220	230	240	250	260	270	280	290	300
310	320	330	340	350	360	370	380	390	400
410	420	430	440	450	460	470	480	490	500
510	520	530	540	550	560	570	580	590	600
610	620	630	640	650	660	670	680	690	700
710	720	730	740	750	760	770	780	790	800
810	820	830	840	850	860	870	880	890	900
910	920	930	940	950	960	970	980	990	1000

Challenge 2 0·1–10 number square

0·1	0·2	0·3	0·4	0·5	0·6	0·7	0·8	0·9	1
1·1	1·2	1·3	1·4	1·5	1·6	1·7	1·8	1·9	2
2·1	2·2	2·3	2·4	2·5	2·6	2·7	2·8	2·9	3
3·1	3·2	3·3	3·3	3·5	3·6	3·7	3·8	3·9	4
4·1	4·2	4·3	4·4	4·5	4·6	4·7	4·8	4·9	5
5·1	5·2	5·3	5·4	5·5	5·6	5·7	5·8	5·9	6
6·1	6·2	6·3	6·4	6·5	6·6	6·7	6·8	6·9	7
7·1	7·2	7·3	7·4	7·5	7·6	7·7	7·8	7·9	8
8·1	8·2	8·3	8·4	8·5	8·6	8·7	8·8	8·9	9
9·1	9·2	9·3	9·4	9·5	9·6	9·7	9·8	9·9	10

Challenge 2 0·01–1 number square

0·01	0·02	0·03	0·04	0·05	0·06	0·07	0·08	0·09	0·1
0·11	0·12	0·13	0·14	0·15	0·16	0·17	0·18	0·19	0·2
0·21	0·22	0·23	0·24	0·25	0·26	0·27	0·28	0·29	0·3
0·31	0·32	0·33	0·33	0·35	0·36	0·37	0·38	0·39	0·4
0·41	0·42	0·43	0·44	0·45	0·46	0·47	0·48	0·49	0·5
0·51	0·52	0·53	0·54	0·55	0·56	0·57	0·58	0·59	0·6
0·61	0·62	0·63	0·64	0·65	0·66	0·67	0·68	0·69	0·7
0·71	0·72	0·73	0·74	0·75	0·76	0·77	0·78	0·79	0·8
0·81	0·82	0·83	0·84	0·85	0·86	0·87	0·88	0·89	0·9
0·91	0·92	0·93	0·94	0·95	0·96	0·97	0·98	0·99	1

Challenge 3 100–1 number square

100	99	98	97	96	95	94	93	92	91
90	89	88	87	86	85	84	83	82	81
80	79	78	77	76	75	74	73	72	71
70	69	68	67	66	65	64	63	62	61
60	59	58	57	56	55	54	53	52	51
50	49	48	47	46	45	44	43	42	41
40	39	38	37	36	35	34	33	32	31
30	29	28	27	26	25	24	23	22	21
20	19	18	17	16	15	14	13	12	11
10	9	8	7	6	5	4	3	2	1

Challenge 3 10–0·1 number square

10	9·9	9·8	9·7	9·6	9·5	9·4	9·3	9·2	9·1
9	8·9	8·8	8·7	8·6	8·5	8·4	8·3	8·2	8·1
8	7·9	7·8	7·7	7·6	7·5	7·4	7·3	7·2	7·1
7	6·9	6·8	6·7	6·6	6·5	6·4	6·3	6·2	6·1
6	5·9	5·8	5·7	5·6	5·5	5·4	5·3	5·2	5·1
5	4·9	4·8	4·7	4·6	4·5	4·4	4·3	4·2	4·1
4	3·9	3·8	3·7	3·6	3·5	3·4	3·3	3·2	3·1
3	2·9	2·8	2·7	2·6	2·5	2·4	2·3	2·2	2·1
2	1·9	1·8	1·7	1·6	1·5	1·4	1·3	1·2	1·1
1	0·9	0·8	0·7	0·6	0·5	0·4	0·3	0·2	0·1

- For each grid, write two or three numbers, making sure that you write the numbers in the correct positions as located on the appropriate number square.

Notes for the children

- Ensure children understand that each of the grids is a different section from a specific number square. Some of the numbers have been given, and they have to work out which numbers belong in the empty squares.

Whole-class, group or individual activities

Example of differentiation content

Challenge 1

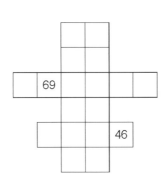

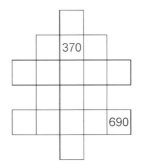

Variations

- If necessary, provide children with the appropriate number square to consult.
- Provide the children with more numbers already on the grid.

Challenge 2

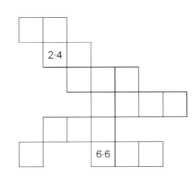

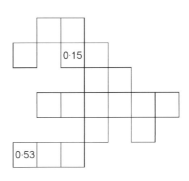

Challenge 3

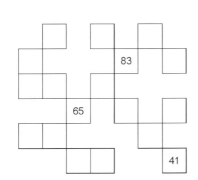

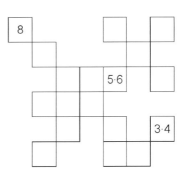

Variations

- Provide the children with fewer numbers already on the grid.
- Provide the children with one of the grids with no numbers on it and ask them to write three or four numbers on it to make their own 'Order the numbers' grid for a friend to solve.

Whole-class, group or individual activities

Across and up

Addition and subtraction

Multiplication

Notes for the teacher

- This activity is ideal for practising and consolidating the concepts of 1, 10 or 100 more or less.
- For each grid write:
  - a number in the grey box
  - an operation (addition, subtraction or multiplication symbol followed by a number) on each of the arrows
  - two or three answers in the other boxes on the grid.
- The first **Challenge 3** example below involves multiplication. Ensure that children are able to use known multiplication facts to mentally calculate the answers needed to complete the grid.
- The second **Challenge 3** example below does not include the number in the grey box nor the operations. Children need to identify the operations and apply the rule to work out the missing numbers.
- When children have completed the grids, discuss with them any patterns and relationships they notice.

Notes for the children

- Ensure children understand that to complete each grid they start with the number in the grey box and to this number they perform the operations given on the arrows, writing the answers in the appropriate boxes on the grid. They continue across and up the grid performing subsequent operations on the previous numbers written on the boxes, for example:

47	76	105	**134**
33	62	91	120
19	48	77	106
5	**34**	63	92

↑ +14

→ +29

Whole-class, group or individual activities

Example of differentiation content

Challenge 1

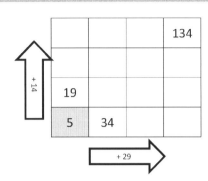

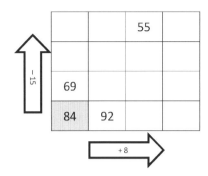

Variations

- Only include calculations that involve adding or subtracting combinations of 1- and 2-digit numbers.
- Provide the children with more answers already on each grid.

Challenge 2

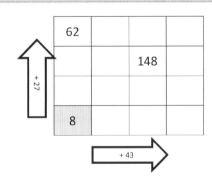

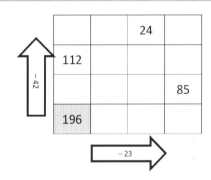

Challenge 3

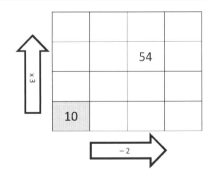

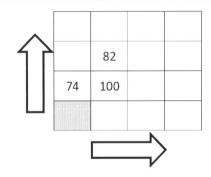

Variations

- Provide the children with fewer (or no) answers already on each grid.
- Include calculations that involve adding or subtracting large numbers or decimals.
- Include calculations that involve using multiplication facts for multiplication tables up to 12 × 12.
- Provide the children with grids with operations written on them, but no numbers in the grey boxes. The children write in their own numbers in the grey boxes and then complete the grids.

Calculations grid (small)

Calculations grid (large)

Addition and subtraction

Multiplication

Notes for the teacher

- There are two versions of this activity. The three examples given below are for the 'Calculations grid (small)' version. However, the same principles apply to the 'Calculations grid (large)' version.

- For each grid write:
  - the addition, subtraction or multiplication symbol in the grey box in the top left-hand corner of the grid
  - numbers in each of the boxes in the top row and the left-hand column of the grid
  - two or three of the answers on the grid.

- Note that for the **Challenge 3** example on page 153, teachers need to complete the grid and then carefully delete some of the answers and numbers in the top row and left-hand column, ensuring that the numbers remaining are sufficient for the children to fill in all the missing numbers on the grid. This version helps children develop their understanding of the inverse relationship between addition and subtraction, and multiplication and division.

- When children have completed the grids, discuss with them any patterns and relationships they notice.

Notes for the children

- Ensure children understand that to complete each grid they start with the number in the left-hand column of the grid, perform the operation given in the grey box then add, subtract or multiply the number in the top row, writing the answer in the appropriate box on the grid.

−	48	23	37	16
57	9	34	20	41
92	44	69	55	76
64	16	41	27	48
83	35	60	46	67

- Although it makes no difference for grids involving addition or multiplication (commutative law), for subtraction grids, it is important that children get into the habit of always starting with the numbers down the left-hand column rather than the numbers in the top row.

Example of differentiation content

 Challenge 1

+	72	19	53	86
34	106			
25				
68		87		
47				

Variations

- Only include calculations that involve adding or subtracting combinations of 1- and 2-digit numbers.
- Provide the children with more answers already on each grid.

 Challenge 2

−	48	23	37	16
57	9			
92				
64			27	
83				

Challenge 3

+	4·5		6·9	
	11·7			
3·8		12		
9·1				14·4
			8·5	

Variations

- Provide the children with fewer (or no) answers already on each grid.
- Include calculations that involve adding or subtracting large numbers or decimals.
- Include calculations that involve using multiplication facts for multiplication tables up to 12 x 12, including multiplying the numbers 1 to 12 by multiples of 10 from 20 to 120, and by decimals from 0·2 to 1·2.

Calculation boxes

Addition

Multiplication

Notes for the teacher

- For each grid write:
    - four numbers in the boxes as shown in the **Challenge 1** and **Challenge 2** examples on page 155
    - the addition or multiplication symbol in the circle at the top.
- Note that for the **Challenge 3** example, teachers need to complete the grid and then carefully delete some of the numbers, ensuring that the numbers remaining are sufficient for the children to fill in all the missing numbers on the grid. This version helps children develop their understanding of the inverse relationship between addition and subtraction, and multiplication and division.
- When children have completed the grids, discuss with them any patterns and relationships they notice.

Notes for the children

- Ensure children understand that to complete each grid they:
    - add (or multiply) pairs of numbers in each row, for example, 4·6 + 2·8 = 7·4 and 3·5 + 2·4 = 5·9, writing the answers in the appropriate spaces
    - add (or multiply) pairs of numbers in each column, for example, 4·6 + 3·5 = 8·1 and 2·8 + 2·4 = 5·2, writing the answers in the appropriate spaces
    - add (or multiply) the two answers in the right-hand column, i.e. 7·4 + 5·9 = 13·3 and write this answer in the grey box.

- If they are correct, this is also the answer to the sum (or product) of the two numbers in the bottom row, i.e. 8·1 + 5·2 = 13·3.
- Note that children can complete the final part of the activity by adding (or multiplying) the two answers in the bottom row first, writing this answer in the grey box, and then adding (or multiplying) the two answers in the right-hand column to check.

+		
4·6	2·8	7·4
3·5	2·4	5·9
8·1	5·2	13·3

Whole-class, group or individual activities

Example of differentiation content

 Challenge 1

 +

56	34	
35	29	

Variations

- Only include calculations that involve adding combinations of 1- and 2-digit numbers.
- Provide the children with the final total in the grey box.

 Challenge 2

 +

4·6	2·8	
3·5	2·4	

 Challenge 3

 ×

6		54
	3	
24		

Variations

- Include calculations that involve adding large numbers or decimals.
- Include calculations that involve using multiplication facts for multiplication tables up to 12 × 12, including multiplying the numbers 1 to 12 by multiples of 10 from 20 to 120, and by decimals from 0·2 to 1·2, for example:

 ×

0·8	7	5·6
4	0·4	1·6
3·2	2·8	8·96

Calculation strips

Addition and subtraction

Multiplication and division

Notes for the teacher

- For each strip write:
  - an operation (addition, subtraction, multiplication or division symbol followed by a number) in the circle
  - a number in each of the boxes down the left-hand side of the strip;
  - one or two answers down the right-hand side of the strip.
- The star at the bottom of each strip can either be used for the children to write their score out of 10, or if you are timing the activity, the time it took them to complete it.
- Note that for the **Challenge 3** example, teachers need to complete the strip and then delete one number from either the left- or right-hand side of the strip. Children need to identify the operation and apply the rule to work out the missing numbers. This version also helps children develop their understanding of the inverse relationship between addition and subtraction, or multiplication and division.
- Also note that, for 'Calculation strips' involving division, depending on what numbers you use, children may have answers with remainders.
- When children have completed the strips, discuss with them any patterns and relationships they notice.

Notes for the children

- Ensure children understand that to complete each strip, they perform the operation given in the circle on each of the ten numbers down the left-hand side of the strip, writing each answer in the box to the right.

41	4
59	22
85	48

(−37)

Whole-class, group or individual activities

Example of differentiation content

Challenge 1

×60	
5	
10	
4	
12	
7	
9	540
11	
6	
3	
8	

☆

Variations

- Only include calculations that involve adding or subtracting combinations of 1- and 2-digit numbers.
- Provide the children with several answers down the right-hand side of the strip.

Challenge 2

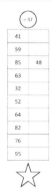

− 37	
41	
59	
85	48
63	
32	
52	
64	
82	
76	
95	

☆

Challenge 3

○	
	2·8
	5·6
3	
7	
12	8·4
5	
	7·7
2	
	4·2
9	

☆

Variations

- Don't provide the children with any answers down the right-hand side of the strip.
- Include calculations that involve adding or subtracting large numbers or decimals.
- Include calculations that involve using multiplication facts for multiplication tables up to 12 x 12, including multiplying the numbers 1 to 12 by multiples of 10 from 20 to 120, and by decimals from 0·2 to 1·2.

Whole-class, group or individual activities

Calculation walls

Addition and subtraction

Multiplication

Notes for the teacher

- For each wall write:
  - three numbers in the 'bricks' as shown in the **Challenge 1** and **Challenge 2** examples below and on page 159
  - the operation (+ or −) in the circle at the top.
- Note the following:
  - For the **Challenge 3** example, teachers need to complete the wall and then carefully delete some of the numbers, ensuring that the numbers remaining are sufficient for the children to fill in all the missing numbers on the wall. This version helps children develop their understanding of the inverse relationship between addition and subtraction, and multiplication and division.
  - For 'Calculation walls' involving subtraction, children need to see subtraction as *finding the difference.*
- When children have completed the walls, discuss with them any patterns and relationships they notice.

Notes for the children

- Ensure children understand that to complete each wall they:
  - add (subtract) adjacent pairs of numbers in the bottom row, for example, 4·5 + 2·8 = 7·3 and 2·8 + 5·4 = 8·2, writing the answers in the 'bricks' immediately above each pair of numbers
  - add (subtract) adjacent pairs of numbers in the remaining row(s), for example, 7·3 + 8·2 = 15·5, writing the answer(s) in the 'brick(s)' immediately above this pair / each pair of numbers
  - write the final answer in the 'brick' at the top of each wall.

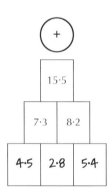

Example of Differentiation Content

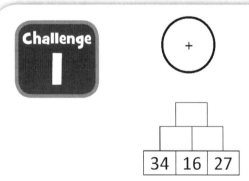

Variations

- Only include calculations that involve adding or subtracting combinations of 1- and 2-digit numbers.
- Provide the children with the final total in the top 'brick'.

Whole-class, group or individual activities

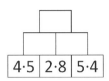

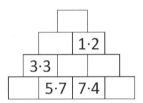

Variations

- Include calculations that involve adding or subtracting large numbers or decimals.
- Where appropriate, discuss with the children how some 'Calculation walls' involving subtraction can have different solutions, for example:

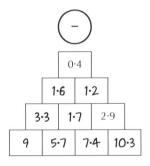 or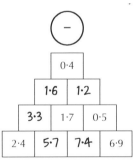

- Use 'Calculation walls' for multiplication.
- For 'Calculation walls' involving multiplication include examples similar to the following. This version helps children develop their understanding of the inverse relationship between multiplication and division.

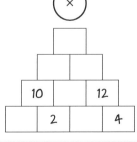

Number chains

Addition and subtraction

Additional resources

- 1–6, 0–9, 1–12 or 1–20 dice (per child)

Notes for the teacher

- For each chain write a number in the grey box.
- This activity can be differentiated not only by the number you write in the grey box, but also by the dice you give the children to use.
- For 'Number chains' involving subtraction ensure that the final answer in the circle will not be a negative number.

Notes for the children

- Children roll the dice, write the number rolled on the line to the right of the grey box, add (subtract) the dice number to (or from) the number in the grey box and write the answer in the first white box.
- The chain continues in this way, with the child rolling the dice, writing the number rolled on the line, adding (subtracting) the dice number to (or from) the number in the previous white box and writing the answer in the next white box.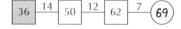
- Each chain finishes when the child writes the final answer in the circle.

Example of differentiation content

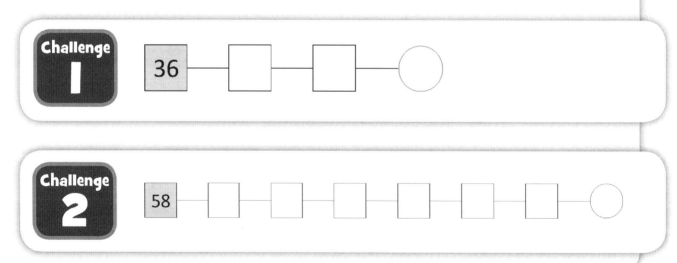

Challenge 3

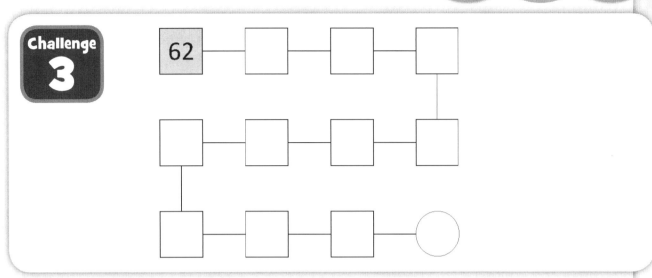

Variations

Challenge 1 Challenge 2 Challenge 3

- Provide children with two 0–9 dice. This will enable them to generate any 2-digit number.

- Write a 2-digit number in the grey boxes and provide the children with a number dice and a six-sided addition and subtraction symbol dice. Children roll both dice and perform the operation generated. Be aware that in some instances children may need to perform calculations across zero.

- Write a decimal in the grey boxes and if available, provide the children with a decimal dice.

Whole-class, group or individual activities

Add and subtract
Add and multiply
Subtract and multiply

Addition and subtraction
Multiplication and division

Notes for the teacher

- There are three versions of this activity. The three examples given below are for the 'Add and subtract' table, however the same principles apply to all three versions.

- These activities are introducing children, in an informal way, to the concept of algebra.

- For each table write:

  − a number in each of the eight boxes below the circle ○

  − a number in each of the eight boxes below the square □.

- Ensure that when using the 'Add and subtract', and 'Subtract and multiply' versions, for each row, you write the larger number in the circle column and the smaller number in the square column.

- The star to the right of each table can either be used for the children to write their score out of 16, or if you are timing the activity, the time it took them to complete it.

- Note that for the **Challenge 3** example, teachers need to complete the table and then delete two numbers from each row of the table. This version helps children develop their understanding of the inverse relationship between addition and subtraction, or multiplication and division. Also note that the example given on page 163 may prove difficult for many children. It is important that before presenting such a table to children that you spend time discussing it with them.

- When children have completed the table, discuss with them any patterns and relationships they notice.

Notes for the children

- Ensure children understand that to complete each table, they perform the operation given in the top row of the third and fourth columns in the table, writing each answer in the appropriate box.

○	□	○ + □	○ − □
81	51	132	30
73	28	101	45
67	30	97	37
64	42	106	22

Example of differentiation content

Challenge 1

◯	☐	◯ + ☐	◯ − ☐
81	51		
73	28		
67	30		
64	42		
59	16		
96	84		
82	35		
73	45		

Variations

- Only include calculations that involve adding or subtracting combinations of 1- and 2-digit numbers.
- Provide the children with several of the answers written in the table.

Challenge 2

◯	☐	◯ + ☐	◯ − ☐
2490	900		
5600	1200		
1310	600		
4250	1800		
6730	3500		
3160	2600		
7520	5700		
8840	4300		

Challenge 3

◯	☐	◯ + ☐	◯ − ☐
5·2	4·3		
6·3		11·4	
9·1		15·3	
3·8			2
2·5			1·5
	2·6	7·5	
		11·9	4·9
		10	5·2

Variations

- Include calculations that involve adding or subtracting large numbers or decimals.
- Include calculations that involve using multiplication facts for multiplication tables up to 12 x 12, including multiplying the numbers 1 to 12 by multiples of 10 from 20 to 120, and by decimals from 0·2 to 1·2.

Whole-class, group or individual activities

Dice calculations (addition)
Dice calculations (subtraction)
Dice calculations (multiplication)
Dice calculations (division)

Addition and subtraction
Multiplication and division

Additional resources

- two 1–6, 0–9, 1–12 or 1–20 dice, or any combination of two dice (per child)

Notes for the teacher

- There are four versions of this activity – one for each of the four operations. With some exceptions (see below), the same principles apply to all four versions.
- The dice you give the children differentiate this activity.

Notes for the children

- Children roll both dice, writing one number in the square and one in the triangle. They then perform the operation and write the answer in the circle.
- Note the following:
  - For 'Dice calculations (subtraction)' children must write the larger number in the square and the smaller number in the triangle.
  - For 'Dice calculations (division)' children must write the larger number in the square and the smaller number in the triangle. However, this version may not be appropriate for some children as, given the random nature of this activity, most of the division calculations that children will generate will result in the answer having a remainder.

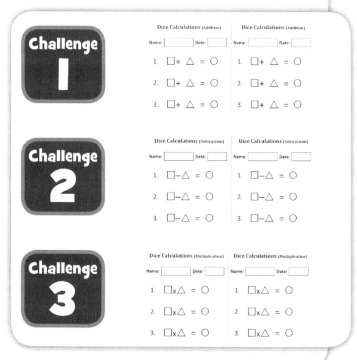

Variations

- For 'Dice calculations (addition)':
  - Write a number in each of the ten squares. Provide each child with only one die (or two 0–9 dice to generate 2-digit numbers). Children roll the die, write the number in the triangle, add the two numbers together and write the answer in the circle.
  - Write a number in each of the ten triangles. Provide each child with only one die (or two 0–9 dice to generate 2-digit numbers). Children roll the die, write the number in the square, add the two numbers together and write the answer in the circle.
  - Write a number in each of the ten circles. Provide each child with only one die (or two 0–9 dice to generate 2-digit numbers). Children roll the die and write the number in the square. They then work out what number they need to add to the number in the square to make the total in the circle. They write this number in the triangle. Note that the numbers you write in each of the circles must be larger than the largest number it is possible to roll on the die (if using two 0–9 dice then the number in the circle must be a 3-digit number).
  - Write a number in each of the ten circles. Provide each child with only one die (or two 0–9 dice to generate 2-digit numbers). Children roll the die and write the number in the triangle. They then work out what number they need to add to the number in the triangle to make the total in the circle. They write this number in the square. Note that the numbers you write in each of the circles must be larger than the largest number it is possible to roll on the die (if using two 0–9 dice then the number in the circle must be a 3-digit number).
- For 'Dice calculations (subtraction)':
  - Write a number in each of the ten squares. Provide each child with only one die (or two 0–9 dice to generate 2-digit numbers). Children roll the die, write the number in the triangle, find the difference between the two numbers and write the answer in the circle. Note that the numbers you write in each of the squares must be larger than the largest number it is possible to roll on the die (if using two 0–9 dice then the number in the squares must be a 3-digit number).
  - Write a 1-digit number in each of the ten triangles. Provide each child with two 0–9 dice. Children roll the dice to generate a 2-digit number, write this number in the square, find the difference between the two numbers and write the answer in the circle.
  - Write a number in each of the ten circles. Provide each child with only one die (or two 0–9 dice to generate 2-digit numbers). Children roll the die and write the number in the triangle. They then work out the minuend and write this number in the square.
  - Write a 1-digit number in each of the ten circles. Provide each child with two 0–9 dice. Children roll the dice to generate a 2-digit number and write this number in the square. They then work out the subtrahend and write this number in the triangle.
- For 'Dice calculations (multiplication)':
  - Write one of the numbers 2–12 in each of the ten squares. Provide each child with one 1–12 die. Children roll the die, write the number in the triangle, multiply the two numbers together and write the product in the circle.
  - Write one of the numbers 2–12 in each of the ten triangles. Provide each child with one 1–12 die. Children roll the die, write the number in the square, multiply the two numbers together and write the product in the circle.
  - Write a 2-digit number, a multiple of 10 or 100, or a decimal in the squares or triangles and provide each child with a 1–12 dice.

16 / 49 / 100 calculations (1-digit numbers)
16 / 49 / 100 calculations (numbers 1–12)
16 / 49 / 100 calculations (2-digit numbers)
16 / 49 / 100 calculations (3-digit numbers)
16 / 49 / 100 calculations (multiples of 10)
16 calculations (multiples of 100)
49 / 100 calculations (multiples of 10 and 100)
16 / 49 / 100 calculations (multiples of 100 and 1000)
16 / 49 / 100 calculations (tenths)
16 / 49 / 100 calculations (hundredths)

Addition and subtraction

Multiplication and division

Notes for the teacher

- There are 27 versions of this activity:
  - nine versions each requiring the children to perform 16 calculations
  - nine versions each requiring the children to perform 49 calculations
  - nine versions each requiring the children to perform 100 calculations.
- The same principles apply to all versions.
- For each grid write an operation (addition, subtraction or multiplication symbol followed by a number) in the circle.
- The operation you write in the circle differentiates this activity.
- The star at the bottom of each grid can either be used for the children to write their score, or if you are timing the activity, the time it took them to complete it.
- When children have completed the grid, discuss with them any patterns and relationships they notice.

Whole-class, group or individual activities

Notes for the children

- Ensure children understand that to complete each grid, they perform the operation given in the circle on the number written in the top left-hand corner of each box, writing each answer in the appropriate box.

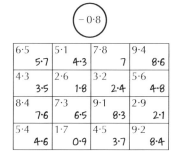

×7			
10 70	3 21	7 49	5 35
6 42	11 77	1 7	4 28
8 56	2 14	9 63	7 49
10 70	1 7	5 35	11 77

- Note that for activities involving subtraction, for example, (− 0·8), ensure children subtract the number in the circle from the number written in the top left-hand corner of each box.

− 0·8			
6·5 5·7	5·1 4·3	7·8 7	9·4 8·6
4·3 3·5	2·6 1·8	3·2 2·4	5·6 4·8
8·4 7·6	7·3 6·5	9·1 8·3	2·9 2·1
5·4 4·6	1·7 0·9	4·5 3·7	9·2 8·4

(continued)

Challenge 1

Challenge 2

Challenge 3

Fluency in Number Facts | Years 5 & 6

49 Calculations (One-digit numbers)

Name: _____ Date: _____

7	9	4	8	1	2	5
3	6	2	1	3	3	5
8	4	7	9	6	2	4
9	3	5	7	1	8	5
2	4	6	8	3	7	1
9	2	7	4	1	8	5
6	9	3	7	5	3	9

49 Calculations (One-digit numbers)

Name: _____ Date: _____

7	9	4	8	1	2	5
3	6	2	1	3	3	5
8	4	7	9	6	2	4
9	3	5	7	1	8	5
2	4	6	8	3	7	1
9	2	7	4	1	8	5
6	9	3	7	5	3	9

Whole-class, paired or individual activities

Variations

- Below is a list of suggestions as to possible operations to write. However, this list must not in any way be seen as the limits that are possible with these activities.

  - 1-digit numbers: ± 1, + 2, + 3, + 4, + 5...; ± 0·1, ± 0·2, ± 0·3, ± 0·4, ± 0·5... ± 0·9; × 2, × 3, × 4... × 99; × 20, × 30, × 40... × 120; × 0·2, × 0·3, × 0·4... × 1·2; × 10; × 100; × 1000; ÷ 10; ÷ 100; ÷ 1000

  - Numbers 1–12: ± 1, + 2, + 3, + 4, + 5...; ± 0·1, ± 0·2, ± 0·3, ± 0·4, ± 0·5... ± 0·9; × 2, × 3, × 4... ; × 20, × 30, × 40... × 120; × 0.2, × 0.3, × 0.4... × 1.2; × 10; × 100; × 1000; ÷ 10; ÷ 100; ÷ 1000

  - 2-digit numbers: + 1, + 2, + 3, + 4, + 5...; − 1, − 2, − 3, − 4, − 5... − 13; ± 10, + 20, + 30, + 40, + 50...; ± 0·1, ± 0·2, ± 0·3, ± 0·4, ± 0·5... ± 1·3; × 2, × 3, × 4... × 12; × 20, × 30, × 40... × 120; × 0·2, × 0·3, × 0·4... × 1·2; × 10; × 100; × 1000; ÷ 10; ÷ 100; ÷ 1000

  - 3-digit numbers: + 1, + 2, + 3, + 4, + 5...; − 1, − 2, − 3, − 4, − 5... − 106; + 10, + 20, + 30, + 40, + 50...; − 10, − 20, − 30, − 40, − 50... − 100; × 10, × 100, × 1000; ÷ 10; ÷ 100; ÷ 1000

  - Multiples of 10: + 1, + 2, + 3, + 4, + 5 ...; − 1, − 2, − 3, − 4, − 5... − 10; + 10, + 20, + 30, + 40, + 50...; × 2, × 3, × 4... × 12; × 10; × 100; × 1000; ÷ 10; ÷ 100; ÷ 1000

  - Multiples of 100 (16 calculations version only): ± 1, ± 2, ± 3, ± 4, ± 5... ± 99; ± 10, ± 20, ± 30, ± 40... ± 100; × 2, × 3, × 4... × 12; × 10; × 100; × 1000; ÷ 10; ÷ 100; ÷ 1000

  - Multiples of 10 and 100 ('49 calculations' and '100 calculations' versions only): + 1, + 2, + 3, + 4, + 5 ...; − 1, − 2, − 3, − 4, − 5... − 10; + 10, + 20, + 30, + 40, + 50...; + 100, + 110, + 120... + 190, + 200, + 210, + 220, + 230 ...; × 2, × 3, × 4... × 12; × 10; × 100; × 1000; ÷ 10; ÷ 100; ÷ 1000

  - Multiples of 100 and 1000: + 1, + 2, + 3, + 4, + 5...; − 1, − 2, − 3, − 4, − 5 ... − 99; + 10, + 20, + 30, + 40, + 50...; − 10, − 20, − 30, − 40, − 50... − 100; + 100, + 110, + 120... + 190, + 200, + 210, + 220, + 230...; + 1000, + 2000, + 3000, + 4000...; × 2, × 3, × 4... × 12; × 10; × 100; ÷ 10; ÷ 100; ÷ 1000

  - Tenths ('16 calculations' and '48 calculations' versions only): ± 1, + 2, + 3, + 4, + 5...; + 0·1, + 0·2, + 0·3, + 0·4, + 0·5 ...; − 0·1, − 0·2, − 0·3, − 0·4, − 0·5... − 1·2; × 2, × 3, × 4 ... × 12; × 10; × 100; × 1000; ÷ 10; ÷ 100

  - Tenths ('100 calculations' version only): ± 1, + 2, + 3, + 4, + 5 ...; ± 0·1, + 0·2, + 0·3, + 0·4, + 0·5...; × 2, × 3, × 4 ... × 12; × 10; × 100; × 1000; ÷ 10; ÷ 100

  - Hundredths: ± 1, + 2, + 3, + 4, + 5 ...; ± 0·1, + 0·2, + 0·3, + 0·4, + 0·5...; + 0·01, + 0·02, + 0·03, + 0·04, + 0·05...; − 0·01, − 0·02, − 0·03, − 0·04, − 0·05... − 0·16; × 2, × 3, × 4... × 10; × 100; × 1000; ÷ 10

Challenge 1
- Provide children with the nine versions that require them to perform 16 calculations.

Challenge 3
- Provide children with the nine versions that require them to perform 100 calculations.

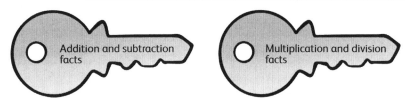

Mental fluency challenges

Objectives

- Add and subtract numbers mentally with increasingly large numbers and decimals
- Recall and use multiplication and division facts for multiplication tables up to 12 × 12
- Multiply and divide numbers mentally drawing upon known facts
- Multiply and divide whole numbers and those involving decimals by 10, 100 and 1000

Teacher resources

Mental fluency
challenges

- scissors

Pupil resources

- 'Mental fluency challenge' (per child)
- pencil (per child)

Introduction

- *Fluency in Number Facts: Years 5 & 6* includes 36 graded 'Mental fluency challenges':
- 18 for Year 5:
- 18 for Year 6:

These challenges are aimed at providing children with further practise and consolidation and also at offering teachers a means of assessing individual children's proficiency in the mental recall of number facts. They can be used with the whole class, specific groups or individual children.

Each challenge covers the key addition, subtraction, multiplication and division number facts that children need to be able to recall instantly by the end of Upper Key Stage 2.

Careful consideration has been given to the progression of the Upper Key Stage 2 curriculum, and for each year group the 18 challenges have been arranged into three different ability levels, with six exercises at each level: **Challenge 1** easy, **Challenge 2** average and **Challenge 3** challenging.

It is recommended that children do the same exercise on two or three consecutive days. This way, the majority of children will see themselves making progress over the two or three days, thus providing greater encouragement and self-motivation.

It is envisaged that these exercises could be given to the children either where they take as long as they need to answer all 15 questions, or as a timed exercise (for example: *I want you to answer as many of these questions as you can in eight minutes. Ready? Go!*). Alternatively, to encourage speed and recall, set the children to work and as they finish the exercise they raise their hand and you tell them how long it took them to complete it.

Both PDF and WORD versions of the 'Mental fluency challenges' are provided.

The WORD version is provided so that individual schools or classes can modify the content of the challenges to better suit the needs of their children. However, it is important to be aware that, if changes are made to the content, the continuity and progression of the challenges will be affected.

The answers to each of the challenges are provided as individual PDF files. Teachers may want to use these to display to the children when marking and discussing the challenges.

(continued)

Multi-domain activities

Whole-class, group or individual activities

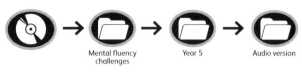

As well as the WORD and PDF versions of the 'Mental fluency challenges', there is also an audio file of each exercise.

A 'Mental fluency challenge answer sheet' is also provided for children to use to record their answers when using the auditory version of the challenges.

To assist with keeping a record of the different 'Mental fluency challenges' that individual children complete throughout the course of a year, a 'Record of mental fluency challenges chart' for Year 5 and Year 6 is also provided. These charts can also be used to record children's scores.

What to do

- Choose an appropriate exercise for the whole class, specific groups or individual children, taking careful consideration of the different needs and abilities of the children. If undertaking the activity with the whole class, you will probably use an exercise from two or three of the different levels: **Challenge 1** easy, **Challenge 2** average or **Challenge 3** challenging.

- If using the WORD / PDF version, distribute the exercise(s) to the children. If using the audio version, ensure that each child has a copy of the 'Mental fluency challenge answer sheet'. Also ensure that each child has a sharpened pencil!

- Allow the children sufficient time to complete the exercise or set the exercise as a timed activity.

- Once the children have completed the exercise, immediately mark the exercise(s), using the relevant PDF answers sheet(s). You may want to mark the challenge(s) with the children's help, asking children to mark their own challenge or swapping and marking someone else's exercise.

- Be sure to discuss the results of the exercise(s) with the children, asking them which questions they found easy, which they found more difficult, and also referring to specific questions, asking them how they worked out the answer. This should provide some excellent data to help identify common errors or misconceptions that children may have. You can then either follow on with some brief impromptu teaching, assisting children to overcome the errors or misconceptions or, alternatively, keep this information in mind for some further teaching at a later date.

- You may want to use the appropriate 'Record of mental fluency challenges chart' to record the exercise that individual children have completed. You may also want to use the chart to record their score.

- And finally...remember to repeat the same exercise on two or three consecutive days.

Paired games and activities

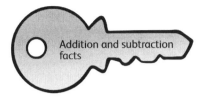

Addition and subtraction facts

Multiplication and division facts

Paired calculations cards

Objectives

- Add and subtract numbers mentally with increasingly large numbers and decimals
- Recall and use multiplication and division facts for multiplication tables up to 12×12
- Multiply and divide numbers mentally drawing upon known facts
- Multiply and divide whole numbers and those involving decimals by 10, 100 and 1000

Teacher resources

Paired games and activities → Paired calculation cards

- 'Paired calculation cards' (ideally printed onto card)

Pupil resources

- Paired calculations card (per pair)

Introduction

Fluency in Number Facts Upper Key Stage 2 includes 36 graded 'Paired calculations cards':

- 18 for Year 5: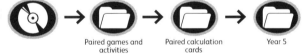

  Paired games and activities → Paired calculation cards → Year 5

- 18 for Year 6: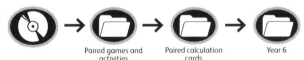

  Paired games and activities → Paired calculation cards → Year 6

Each card covers the key addition, subtraction, multiplication and division number facts that children need to be able to recall instantly by the end of Upper Key Stage 2.

Careful consideration has been given to the progression of the Upper Key Stage 2 curriculum, and for each year group the 18 cards have been arranged into three different ability levels, with six cards at each level: **Challenge 1** easy, **Challenge 2** average and **Challenge 3** difficult.

It is recommended that pairs of children use the same card on two or three consecutive days. This way, the majority of children will see themselves making progress over the two or three days, thus providing greater encouragement and self-motivation.

(continued)

Assessment & record-keeping formats

To assist with keeping a record of the different 'Paired calculations cards' that individual children complete throughout the course of a year, a 'Record of paired calculations cards chart' for Year 5 and Year 6 is also provided.

What to do

- Arrange the children into pairs of similar ability.
- Provide each pair with an appropriate card, taking careful consideration of the different needs and abilities of the children: **Challenge 1** easy, **Challenge 2** average or **Challenge 3** difficult.
- Each pair positions the card between them with one child having a clear view of Side A and the other child a clear view of Side B.
- Children take turns to ask their partner the 15 questions on their side of the card. Ensure the children realise that they do not say the answer in the grey box. You may also need to demonstrate to the children how to phrase questions such as 12 + [?] = 30, i.e. *Twelve add what other number equals 30?* and [?] – 8 = 26, i.e. *What number, minus 8, equals 26?*
- As each child says an answer, their partner responds saying whether the answer is correct or not.
- Once each child has asked their partner the 15 questions on their side of the card, the children turn the card around and repeat.
- When pairs have finished be sure to discuss the results with the children, asking them which questions they found easy, which they found more difficult, and also referring to specific questions, asking them how they worked out the answer. This will probably provide some excellent data in helping identify common errors or misconceptions that children may have, which you can then either follow on with some brief impromptu teaching, assisting children to overcome the errors or misconceptions, or alternatively keeping this information in mind for some further teaching at a later date.
- You may want to use the appropriate 'Record of paired calculations cards chart' to record the card that pairs of children have completed.
- And finally…remember to ask pairs of children to use the same card on two or three consecutive days.

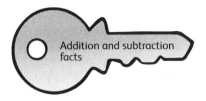

Function Machine

Objectives

- Add and subtract numbers mentally with increasingly large numbers and decimals
- Recall and use multiplication and division facts for multiplication tables up to 12×12
- Multiply and divide numbers mentally drawing upon known facts
- Multiply and divide whole numbers and those involving decimals by 10, 100 and 1000

Teacher resources

- none

Pupil resources

- 'Function machine' (My Maths Function Machine, B&W or colour version) printed onto card (per child)
- 'Function Machine' strip (per child)

Introduction

Fluency in Number Facts Upper Key Stage 2 includes 36 graded 'Function Machine' strips:

- 18 for Year 5:

- 18 for Year 6:

Each 'Function Machine' strip covers the key addition, subtraction, multiplication and division number facts that children need to be able to recall instantly by the end of Upper Key Stage 2.

Careful consideration has been given to the progression of the Upper Key Stage 2 curriculum, and for each year group the 18 strips have been arranged into three different ability levels, with six strips at each level: **Challenge 1** easy, **Challenge 2** average and **Challenge 3** difficult.

It is recommended that children use the same strip on several consecutive days – perhaps even for a whole week. This way, the majority of children will see themselves making progress, thus providing greater encouragement and self-motivation.

(continued)

It is recommended that before children do the 'Function machine strip' activity for the first time, that you provide each child with a copy of the 'Function machine' ('My Maths Function Machine') which is printed onto card for the children to personalise.

Assessment & record-keeping formats

To assist with keeping a record of the different 'Function Machine' strips that individual children complete throughout the course of a year, a 'Record of Function Machine strips' chart for Year 5 and Year 6 is also provided.

What to do

- Provide each child with an appropriate strip, taking careful consideration of the different needs and abilities of the children: **Challenge 1** easy, **Challenge 2** average or **Challenge 3** challenging.

- Children carefully feed the strip through their function machine, only revealing one calculation at a time.

- The child works out the answer and then moves the strip on slightly to reveal the answer.

- Children continue in this way until they get to the end of the strip and the tenth answer is revealed.

- Encourage the children to use the same strip several times in one session – aiming to make fewer errors and / or to complete the strip in a shorter period of time.

- When individual children have finished, you may want to ask them which questions they found easy, which they found more difficult, and also referring to specific questions, ask them how they worked out the answer. This should provide some excellent data in helping identify common errors or misconceptions that children may have, which you can then either follow on with some brief impromptu teaching, assisting children to overcome the errors or misconceptions, or alternatively keeping this information in mind for some further teaching at a later date.

- You may want to use the appropriate 'Record of Function Machine strips' chart to record the strips that individual children have completed.

- And finally…remember to ask the children to use the same strip on several consecutive days.